Samatvam

BIHAR SCHOOL OF YOGA

50 years

1963–2013
GOLDEN JUBILEE

WORLD YOGA CONVENTION 2013
GANGA DARSHAN, MUNGER, BIHAR, INDIA
23rd–27th October 2013

Samatvam

The Yoga of Equanimity

From the teachings of Swami Sivananda Saraswati
and Swami Satyananda Saraswati

Yoga Publications Trust, Munger, Bihar, India

Published by Yoga Publications Trust
   First edition 2009
   Reprinted 2012

ISBN: 978-81-86336-78-6

Publisher and distributor: Yoga Publications Trust, Ganga Darshan, Munger, Bihar, India.

Website: www.biharyoga.net
         www.rikhiapeeth.net

Printed at Thomson Press (India) Limited, New Delhi, 110001

Dedication

In humility we offer this dedication to
Swami Sivananda Saraswati, who initiated
Swami Satyananda Saraswati into the secrets of yoga.

Contents

Introduction

This book is compiled from the teachings of Swami Sivananda Saraswati and Swami Satyananda Saraswati. It addresses one of the most revered spiritual virtues, samatvam. *Samatvam* means complete equanimity within oneself and with everybody else, with Nature and with the whole cosmos. It is the state where one's entire being becomes calm and quiet and one is able to think, to decide and to solve the problems of life with absolute tranquillity.

Samatvam, the yoga of peace, contentment, equanimity and balance of mind, is a vital need for everyone, whether involved in household life, in business, in politics or in spiritual sadhana. It is an absolute necessity for anyone subjected to the wear and tear of tensions, frustrations and disappointments. It is a basic requirement for the spiritual aspirant trying to develop his higher faculties, and even for those who aspire to samadhi and the highest states of consciousness. Anyone trying to live a fulfilling life must know how to maintain equanimity under all circumstances and be able to sustain the calmness inherent in that state of mind.

These teachings are full of scriptural references and the revelations of two modern day yogis who have mastered the requisites of samatvam. Their teachings present samatvam as a process of accepting life as it is given, and knowing how to utilize every moment of existence as a means to evolve one's consciousness. Their wisdom echoes the eternal spiritual truths that enlighten humankind's quest to conquer mental and emotional turmoil, that show the way out of entanglement with endless sensual desires and the entrenched idiosyncrasies of the human psyche.

The words of these yogis are an inspiration to improve our quality of awareness, our faith, and our relationships with each and every thing around us. They emphasize that we must sustain a balance between our external and internal worlds; that we should not be all intellect or all emotion, but rather a perfect blend of both. Otherwise, we will have no lasting peace or contentment in life. They show us the ways to uplift and purify our minds, hearts and actions through the practices of selfless service, bhakti and yoga. They tell us of the traditional yogic techniques that will gradually introvert the mind and allow us to experience the stillness and silence of our very own soul. And they encourage us to seek the company of saints and sages so as to understand why worldly life can never give supreme serenity.

The reader is given the very clear message that to attain the supreme peace of the Eternal there is no need to flee from one's worldly career and hide in a Himalayan cave. Rather, learn to resist unrighteousness, develop divine virtues, and try to attain Self-realization in and through the world. One is to be ever active and at the same time feel inwardly that one is the non-doer and non-enjoyer. Take a deep interest in everything, and yet remain perfectly unattached.

In the words of Swami Satyananda, "Man is the most beautiful and privileged creation of God. His glory is that he can sublimate his natural and irresistible urges for possessions and sensual enjoyments, and transform himself into something noble and divine. And yet, although our ultimate, eternal abode is the seat of Brahman, we are all pilgrims here, and pain and pleasure will come our way. The clouds of calamities may eclipse our inner shrine, but with nothing should we barter the peace of our soul. Only one who considers pain and pleasure as passing phenomena and is always aware of his goal will be really happy."

Samatvam

From the teachings of Swami Sivananda Saraswati

1

The Yoga of Equanimity

Perform action, O Arjuna, being steadfast in yoga, abandoning attachment and balanced in success or failure. Such equanimity is called yoga.

Bhagavad Gita (2:48)

Samatvam is equanimity of mind and outlook, equipoise. It is being able to keep the mind steady and balanced in all the conditions of life. It is the ability to be forever serene, contented, calm and peaceful. Samatvam is having the ability to remain cheerful in adverse conditions, to have fortitude in meeting danger, and to have the presence of mind and forbearance to bear insult, injury and persecution. Samatvam means being able to go through the routine of life, amidst the din and clamour of the world, patiently and joyfully.

Samatvam is the yoga that Lord Krishna talks about at length in the *Bhagavad Gita*. He defines yoga as: *Samatvam yoga uchyate* (2:48): Samatvam is yoga; equanimity is yoga. Lord Krishna considers samatvam as that evenness of mind which is upheld by a true yogi amidst the worst of all difficulties, turmoil and calamities; as that state wherein all the mental modifications, thoughts, imaginations, whims, fancies, moods, impulses, emotions and instincts are transcended. He explains that samatvam is being able to maintain one's balance of mind in success and failure, gain and loss, pleasure and pain, and that it is the aptitude of a perfect master who remains equipoised in all circumstances. That is samatvam, the yoga of equanimity.

The definition of samatvam goes far beyond the temporary condition of mental quietude which people speak of when they retire for a short time to a Himalayan hermitage, or to the Alps, or to a quiet nature reserve for a little rest when they are tired after a long journey. Samatvam is the attainment of absolute peace and tranquillity of the highest calibre. It is the realm of serenity where the cares, worries, anxieties and fears which torment the soul dare not enter. Samatvam is the realm of eternal sunshine where all distinctions of caste, creed and colour disappear in the warm embrace of divine love and where desires and cravings have found their full satiety.

Everyone in the world is restless and striving after something, but exactly what he does not know. He feels he is in need of something, the nature of which he does not comprehend. He gets degrees, diplomas, titles, honour, power, name and fame. He marries, begets children. In short, he gets all that he supposes would give him happiness. A person may possess immense wealth, all sorts of comforts and an easy going life, yet he will have no peace of mind because he has no inner harmony. There is discord in his heart due to greed, selfishness, egoism, lust, pride, fear, hatred, anger and worry. He finds that worldly greatness, when secured, is a delusion and a snare, and finds no peace or happiness in it. Outward harmony and quietness cannot give real peace of mind.

Goal of life

Pious people, saints and sages declare that the restlessness afflicting everyone, the state of discontent, discomfort and dissatisfaction, and the feeling of being ill at ease with oneself and one's surroundings is due to the loss of companionship with one's soul. Man has forgotten that the goal of life is the attainment of Self-realization or God-consciousness. There is one supreme, undying intelligent principle or essence,

6

Atman or Brahman or the Supreme Self, who dwells in the chambers of everyone's heart. He exists in the past, present and future. He is existence absolute, knowledge absolute and bliss absolute. Abiding joy or lasting peace can only be obtained if man realizes his own Self through spiritual sadhana, self-restraint, purity and meditation. Ultimately, he must reach the yoga of equanimity.

The yoga of equanimity cannot be found in the acquisition of external objects. Wealth, children, property and palatial buildings cannot give everlasting peace and balance of mind. To attain the divine qualities of samatvam, the aspirant needs to realize his oneness with that one supreme Self, who lives in the silent, still nature within. When he is established in 'That', which is an ocean of peace and happiness, he will not be shaken even by heavy sorrow, loss or failure, inharmonious and disagreeable vibrations. He will be able to tide over all the difficulties or crises of life very easily and triumph in all experiences. Mysterious is this peace! Marvellous is this peace! Realize this peace that transcends all understanding through yoga sadhana, and be free. Float in this ocean of serenity and rejoice in the stillness of your own Self.

Samatvam is an internal state of mind. It can be had without the help of money and outwardly favourable circumstances. One may have sorrows and yet enjoy inward harmony and steadiness of mind if one constantly rests in God by withdrawing the senses, stilling the mind and eradicating its impurities. Lord Jesus was persecuted in a variety of ways. He was put to death on the cross and yet, what did he say? He said, "O Lord, forgive them. They know not what they are doing." How peaceful he was even when his life was at stake! He was enjoying inner peace. No tribulation or calamity could touch him.

Look within

Samatvam can be found only within. Look within. Search for it within the quietness of your mind through one-pointed concentration and meditation. If you do not find peace there, you will not find it anywhere else. Sit silently in a room for half an hour to one hour every day. Close the eyes. Relax the muscles and nerves. Withdraw the senses and the mind from external objects. Forget the body and the world. Concentrate at the space between the eyebrows. Meditate regularly in the early morning hours. Enter into the great calm or the secret place of the most high.

If you wish to enter into the great peace of the soul, all worldly desires must die. Only one who has brought the senses under perfect control and stilled the mind can meditate and rest in the Self and attain perfect equilibrium. The serenity of samatvam lies very close to those who know themselves, who are of a subdued nature and thought. One who is endowed with supreme faith and who has mastery over the senses attains the supreme peace of samatvam quickly.

Equanimity is in that person who has given up 'mineness' and 'I-ness', who has given up egoism, cravings, desires and longing for objects. When this thirst dies, one enjoys the peace of a calm, steady mind. One is perfectly content. Samatvam can be enjoyed only by one who has dispassion, who has understood the magnitude and purpose of human suffering, who knows the real value of life on earth. Samatvam can be had only by one who has understood the worthlessness of perishable objects and the passing powers and positions in this world and has no desire for them.

One who has found out the real purpose of his birth in this world, who yearns for liberation, who has understood that beyond the names and forms there is one eternal, everlasting Atman, and who practises self-discipline, he alone can attain the yoga of equanimity. Such a person is a yogi of the highest order. Real peace of mind does not come from outside. It is produced in the same mind when the mind is controlled and its thoughts are checked. Great efforts must be made to check the passions and desires. Only then will the aptitude for activity be subdued and will one be at rest with the thoughts stilled.

Sincere sadhana

An ordinary worldly-minded person can neither hear the inner voice of the Atman nor attain equipoise of mind. However, it is possible to develop equilibrium or balance of mind by regular and sincere sadhana of japa, selfless service, enquiry into the Self, satsang, meditation, light sattwic food, tapas and self-study. In the world there are people with a few pure virtues such as patience, generosity and forgiveness, but a spiritual aspirant must endeavour to develop his mind as a whole, to acquire all the sattwic virtues. All sadhanas aim at purification of the mind and the attainment of equanimity, and pure, strong determination will pave a long way to achieving that state.

The mind always runs after sensual objects, even though it experiences immense misery, grief, pain and sorrow. It will never give up its old habits. The aspirant will have to captivate this shameless mind and take it to its source, Brahman, by chanting the mantra *Om* with feeling again and again. Let it taste the *ananda*, the infinite bliss of the Atman. Only then will it find its rest in *Om*, its original abode of eternal peace.

2

The Perfectly Balanced Mind

In the *Bhagavad Gita*, Arjuna is eager to know from Lord Krishna the characteristic marks of the person who possesses '. . . ever c alm wisdom, who is steeped in perfect tranquillity of mind . . .'. Lord Krishna enlightens his disciple Arjuna with a wonderful portrait of such a yogi, giving a detailed description of his qualities.

> Endowed with wisdom (evenness of mind), one casts off in this life both good and bad deeds. Therefore, devote yourself to yoga. Yoga is skill in action. (2:50)

Action done with evenness of mind is the yoga of equanimity or wisdom. The sage who is established in this yoga is not affected by success or failure because he does not seek the fruits or results of his actions. His entire existence is established in the Self, and he possesses poised reason. All his actions are performed with equipoise of mind and he thus escapes from all the good and bad results of whatever work he undertakes. He knows that clinging to the fruits of action leads to bondage and that the performer of such actions will have to take birth again and again in this mortal world to work through them. Action performed by one who expects fruits for his actions is far inferior to the yoga of equanimity.

The sage, who performs his work with equanimity of mind, thus performs all actions for the sake of God. He works simply to perform his duty and in doing so he fulfils the purpose of existence. Without the desire for rewards, he is released from the otherwise endless cycle of birth and death. He then attains the blissful state or the immortal abode.

> When your mind crosses beyond the mire of delusion, then you will become indifferent as to what has been heard and what has yet to be heard. (2:52)

The mire of delusion is the identification of the Self with the non-Self. The sense of discrimination between the Self and the non-Self is confounded by the mire of delusion, and the mind runs towards sensual objects and the body is taken as the pure Self. When you attain purity of mind, you will become indifferent to things heard and yet to be heard. You will go beyond the darkness of worldly delusion and become established in the eternal existence of the Self. Worldly enjoyments will appear to you to be of no use, and you will not care a bit for them. You will entertain disgust for them and rise above the pairs of opposites.

> When one completely casts off, O Arjuna, all the desires of the mind and is satisfied in the Self by the Self, then he is said to be one of steady wisdom. (2:55)

If anyone can attain the supreme bliss of the Self, will he thirst for sensual pleasures? No, not at all! If anyone gets sugar candy will he crave for black sugar? Certainly not! The sum total of all the pleasures of the world will seem worthless for the sage of steady wisdom, *sthitaprajna,* who is satisfied in the Self. Even when he is placed in affluent conditions, he does not long for sensual pleasures. These are the marks of a contented man. Those who cling to worldly pleasures and powers to satisfy their sensual cravings cannot have steadiness of mind. They cannot concentrate or meditate on the Self. They are ever busy planning projects for the acquisition of wealth and power to gratify their senses. Their minds are ever restless, impure and unbalanced.

11

He whose mind is not shaken by adversity, who does not hanker after pleasures, and is free from attachment, fear and anger, is called a sage of steady wisdom. (2:56)

The mind of a sage of steady wisdom is not distressed by calamities. He is perfectly balanced under all circumstances. His mind is always cool and unaffected by the *dvandvas*, pairs of opposites. There will be no anger or desire. He is neither elated by enjoyments nor depressed by sorrow and grief. Without being affected by the pleasures or pains of enjoyments though moving in them, the mind of an aspirant will become inured to them.

Through internal contentment and freedom from pain, there will arise in the aspirant a steadiness of mind in all circumstances and in all places. There is not the least longing for objects. His mind is above worldly things. He is not affected by the three afflictions: *adhyatmika*, arising from diseases or disorders in one's own body; *adhidaivika*, arising from thunder, lightning, storms, floods, etc; and *adhibautika*, arising from scorpions, cobras, tigers, etc. Equipped with this attitude of mind, he is able to throw off completely the shackles of all his actions in life.

One who is everywhere without attachment, on meeting with anything good or bad, who neither rejoices nor hates, his wisdom is fixed. (2:57)

The sage who possesses poised understanding or evenness of mind does not rejoice in pleasure nor is he averse to pain that may befall him. He is quite indifferent as he is rooted in the Self. He has no attachments even for his life or body as he identifies himself with Brahman or the Supreme Self. He will not praise anybody who does good to him nor censure anyone who does harm to him.

When, like the tortoise which withdraws its limbs on all sides, the yogi withdraws his senses from the sense objects, then his wisdom becomes steady. (2:58)

Withdrawal of the senses is called *pratyahara* or abstraction. The mind has a natural tendency to run towards external objects. However, the yogi who has attained the state of samatvam is endowed with the ability known as pratyahara. Thus he is always able to withdraw his mind from the objects of the senses within the twinkling of an eye, and fix it on the Self within. As such he is not disturbed by tumultuous sounds and noises of any description. Even on the battlefield he can rest in his centre, the Self, by withdrawing his senses. This sage who practises pratyahara is dead to the world. He will not be affected by any outside vibrations. At any time, by mere willing, he can bring his senses under perfect control. They are his obedient servants or instruments.

> The sense objects turn away from one who abstains, leaving the longing (behind); but his longing also turns away on seeing the Supreme. (2:59)

The yogi who is established in samatvam attains the knowledge of the Self. In doing so, all the *vasanas* or subtle latent tendencies, all the subtle desires, all the subtle attachments and even the longing for objects are completely destroyed. Through attainment of this knowledge of the Self, by the practice of spiritual disciplines, not only have the objects of the senses turned away from the sage, but also the relish or taste or longing for the objects has been annihilated.

> The turbulent senses, O Arjuna, do violently carry away the mind of a wise man though he is striving (to control them). (2:60)

The aspirant should first bring the senses under his control by purifying the mind. The senses are like turbulent horses. If you keep them under perfect control, you can reach your destination safely; otherwise they will throw you down on the way. Like turbulent horses, the turbulent senses will throw you down into the objects of the senses and you will be unable to reach your spiritual destination, the abode of eternal peace and immortality, final liberation. The senses are powerful and continually draw the mind outwards, and you may fail in your initial attempts many, many times. But if you endeavour to keep a balanced mind under all conditions, you will obtain strength and slowly manifest equanimity. Mastery over the mind should become the object of your sadhana. Endowed with equanimity, you will cast off both good and bad in this life.

> Therefore, having restrained all the senses, he should sit steadfast, intent on Me. His wisdom is steady whose senses are under control. (2:61)

The aspirant should control the senses and sit focused on Me as the Supreme, with a calm mind. The wisdom of the yogi who thus seated has brought all his senses under control is doubtlessly quite steady. He is established in the Self.

> When a man thinks of sense objects, attachment for them arises; from attachment desire is born; from desire anger arises. (2:62)

When a man thinks of the beauty and the pleasant and alluring features of the sense objects, he becomes attached to them. He then regards them as something worthy of acquiring and possessing and hankers after them. He develops a strong desire to possess them. Then he endeavours his level best to obtain them. When his desire is frustrated by some cause or other, anger arises in his mind. If anybody places an obstruction in his way of obtaining the objects, he hates him, fights with him and develops hostility towards him.

> From anger comes delusion; from delusion loss of memory; from loss of memory the destruction of discrimination; from the destruction of discrimination he perishes. (2:63)

From anger arises delusion. When a man becomes angry, he loses his power of discrimination between right and wrong. He will speak and do whatever he likes. He will be swept away by the impulse of passion and emotion and will act irrationally. His mind is unbalanced.

> But the self-controlled man, moving among the sense objects with the senses under restraint and free from attraction and repulsion, attains peace. (2:64)

The mind and the senses are naturally endowed with the two currents of attraction and repulsion. Therefore, the mind and the senses like certain objects and dislike certain other objects. But the disciplined man, who moves among the sense objects with the mind and senses free from attraction and repulsion and mastered by the Self, attains eternal peace. The senses and the mind obey his will, as the disciplined self has a very strong will. The disciplined self takes only those objects which are quite necessary for maintenance of the body without any love or hatred. He never takes those objects which are forbidden by the scriptures.

> In that peace all pains are destroyed; for the intellect of the tranquil-minded soon becomes steady. (2:65)

When mental peace is attained, there is no hankering after sense objects. The yogi has perfect mastery over his reason. The intellect abides in the Self, the Atman. It is quite steady. The miseries of the body and the mind come to an end.

> There is no knowledge of the Self for the unsteady; for the unsteady no meditation is possible; for the unmeditative there can be no peace, and for the man who has no peace, how can there be happiness? (2:66)

One who cannot concentrate and fix his mind in meditation cannot have knowledge of the Self. He cannot have the quality of discrimination. The unsteady man cannot practise meditation. Without intense devotion to Self-knowledge and intense longing for liberation or *moksha*, he cannot become established in the Self. One who does not practise meditation cannot possess peace of mind. How can one who has no peace of mind enjoy happiness?

Desire, thirsting for sense objects, is the enemy of peace. There cannot be an iota or tinge of happiness for a man who is thirsting for sensual objects. The mind will be ever restless and hankering after the objects. Only when this thirsting dies, does man enjoy peace. Only then can he meditate and rest in the Self.

> For the mind, which follows in the wake of the wandering senses, carries away discrimination, as the wind (carries away) a boat on the waters. (2:67)

The mind which constantly dwells on sensual objects and moves in company with the senses completely destroys the quality of man's discriminative powers. Just as the wind carries a boat away from its course, so too the mind carries the aspirant away from his spiritual path and turns him towards the objects of the senses.

> Therefore, O Arjuna, his knowledge is steady whose senses are completely restrained from the sense objects. (2:68)

When the senses are completely controlled, the mind cannot wander wildly in sensual grooves. It becomes steady like a lamp in a windless place. The yogi is then established in the Self and his knowledge is steady.

> That which is night to all beings, in that the self-controlled man is awake; when all beings are awake, that is night for the sage who sees. (2:69)

That which is real for worldly-minded people is illusion for the sage, and vice versa. The sage lives in the Self. This is day for him. He is unconscious of worldly phenomena. They are night for him, as it were. The ordinary man is unconscious of his real nature. Life in the spirit is night for him. He is experiencing the objects of sensual enjoyment. This is day for him. The Self is a non-entity for him! For a sage this world is a non-entity.

Worldly minded people are in utter darkness as they have no knowledge of the Self. What is darkness for them is all light for the sage. The Self, Atman or Brahman is night for the worldly minded. But the sage is fully awake. He is directly cognizing the Supreme Reality, the light of lights. He is full of illumination and knowledge of the Self or *atma jnana*.

He into whom all desires enter like water enters the ocean which, although filled from all sides, remains unmoved, he alone attains peace; but not the man who is full of desires. (2:70)

Just as the ocean filled with waters from all sides remains unmoved, so also the sage who is resting in his own essence or Self is not at all affected though desires of all sorts enter from all sides. The sage attains peace or liberation, but not he who longs for objects of sensual enjoyment and entertains various desires.

He attains peace who, abandoning all desires, moves about without longing, without the sense of mine and without egoism. (2:71)

The man who lives destitute of longing, abandoning all desires, without the sense of 'I' and 'mine', who is satisfied with the bare necessities of life, who has no attachment even for the bare necessities of life, attains moksha or eternal peace. One who attains this state is never deluded. What is the secret of yogic action? Even though one is not engaged in action, if the mind is active with the idea of doership and egoism, then it is action in inaction. On the other hand, though engaged physically in intense action, if the idea of agency is absent, if one feels that *Prakriti* or Nature does everything, it is inaction in action. He is unaffected by the pairs of opposites like joy and grief, success and failure. Samatvam can only be achieved when one is free from attachment, fear and anger, being thoroughly purified by right knowledge.

But renunciation, O Arjuna, is hard to attain without yoga; the yoga-harmonized sage quickly goes to Brahman. (5:6)

Brahman here signifies renunciation because renunciation consists of knowledge of the Self. A *muni*, the sage of meditation, the yoga-harmonized sage, is one who has been purified by the performance of action. He quickly attains Brahman, the true renunciation which is devotion to knowledge of the Self. Therefore, karma yoga is better. It is easy for a beginner and prepares him for the higher yoga by purifying his mind.

> He who is devoted to the path of action, whose mind is quite pure, who has conquered the self, who has subdued his senses and who realizes his Self as the Self in all beings, though acting, is not tainted. (5:7)

He who is harmonized by yoga, who has purified his mind by devotion to the performance of action, who has conquered the body and subjugated the senses, whose Self is the Self of all beings, he will not be bound by actions although he performs actions for the wellbeing or protection of the masses in order to set an example to them.

> One who is united (well-poised or harmonized), having abandoned the fruit of action, attains eternal peace; only the non-united (the unsteady or unbalanced), impelled by desire, attached to the fruit, is bound. (5:12)

The harmonious man who does actions for the sake of the Lord without expectation of the fruits and who says, "I do actions for my Lord only, not for my personal gain or profit," attains the peace born of devotion and steadfastness through the following four stages: purity of mind, attainment of knowledge, renunciation of actions, and steadiness in wisdom. But the unbalanced or unharmonized person, who is led by desire, who is attached to the fruits of the actions and who says, "I have done such and such an action; I will get such and such a fruit," is firmly bound.

> Even here (in this world) birth (everything) is overcome by those whose minds rest in equality; Brahman is

18

spotless indeed and equal; therefore they are established in Brahman. (5:19)

When the mind becomes rooted in equanimity or evenness or equality, when it is always in a balanced state, one conquers birth and death. Bondage is annihilated and freedom is attained. When the mind is in a perfectly balanced state, he overcomes Brahman Himself, that is, he realizes Brahman.

Resting in Brahman, with steady intellect and un-deluded, the knower of Brahman neither rejoices on obtaining what is pleasant nor grieves on obtaining what is unpleasant. (5:20)

This is the state of a *jivanmukta* or a liberated sage who identifies with the Self or Atman. He always has a balanced mind. He is never deluded. He has abandoned all actions as he rests in Brahman. He who has an unbalanced mind, who identifies with the body and mind, feels pleasure and pain, exhilaration of spirit when he gets a pleasant object and grief when he obtains an unpleasant object.

He who is able, while still here (in this world) to withstand, before liberation from the body, the impulse born out of desire and anger – he is a yogi, harmonized or steadfast in yoga, he is a happy man. (5:23)

Desire and anger are powerful enemies of peace. It is very difficult to annihilate them. You will have to make very strong efforts to destroy these enemies if you wish to attain the yoga of equanimity. One who has controlled desire and anger is the happiest man in the world.

With the senses, the mind and the intellect (ever) controlled, having liberation as his supreme goal, free from desire, fear and anger – the sage is verily liberated forever. (5:28)

If one is free from desire, fear and anger he enjoys perfect peace of mind. When the senses, the mind and the intellect are subjugated, the sage does constant contemplation and attains forever absolute freedom or moksha. The mind becomes restless when the modifications of desire, fear and anger arise in it. When one becomes desireless, the mind moves towards the Self spontaneously; liberation or moksha becomes his highest goal.

He who knows Me as the enjoyer of sacrifices and austerities, the great Lord of all the worlds and the friend of all beings, attains peace. (5:29)

I am the Lord of all sacrifices and austerities. I am their author, goal and their God. I am the friend of all beings, the doer of good to them without expecting any return for it. I am the dispenser of the fruits of all actions and the silent witness of their minds, thoughts and actions, as I dwell in their hearts. On knowing Me, they attain peace and liberation or moksha, deliverance from birth and death and all worldly miseries and sorrows.

O Arjuna, know yoga to be that which they call renunciation: no one verily becomes a yogi who has not renounced thoughts. (6:2)

Sankalpa is the working of the imagining faculty of the mind which makes plans for the future and guesses the results of plans so formed. Hope, desire and greed make the mind ever restless and turbulent. No one can become a yogi of balanced mind who plans and schemes and expects rewards for his actions. The yogic aspirant should be free from hope, desire and greed. Only then will he have a steady mind. Nor should the aspirant have many possessions. He must only keep those articles which are absolutely necessary for maintenance of his body. If there are many possessions, the mind will be always thinking of them and attempting to protect them. No devotee of action who has not renounced the thought of the fruits of his actions can become a yogi of steady mind. The thought of fruits will certainly make the mind unsteady.

When a man is not attached to sense objects or to actions, having renounced all thoughts, then he is said to have attained yoga. (6:4)

When a yogi, keeping his mind quite steady by withdrawing it from the objects of the senses, has attachment neither for sensual objects such as sound, nor for actions, knowing that they are of no use to him; when he has renounced all thoughts which generate various sorts of desires for the objects of this world and of the next, then he is said to have become established in yoga (of equanimity).

The Supreme Self of one who is self-controlled and peaceful is balanced in cold and heat, pleasure and pain, as also in honour and dishonour. (6:7)

The self-controlled yogi, who is rooted in the Self, maintains poise amidst the pairs of opposites or the alternating waves of cold and heat, pleasure and pain, honour and dishonour. When the yogi has subdued his senses, when his mind is balanced and peaceful under all conditions, when he is not in the least influenced by the pairs of opposites, when he had renounced all actions, then the Highest Self really becomes his own Self. He attains Self-realization. As he rests in his own Self, he is ever serene or tranquil. He remains unshaken, unchanged or unaffected though he comes in contact with the sense objects and he stands adamant in the face of the changing conditions of Nature. He is called the silent witness of the mind, or Brahman.

Serene minded, fearless, firm in the vow of a brahmachari, having controlled the mind, thinking of Me and balanced in mind, let him sit, having Me as his supreme goal. (6:14)

The spiritual aspirant should possess serenity of mind. The divine light can descend only in a serene mind. Serenity is attained by the eradication of desires and cravings. He should be fearless. This is the most important qualification. A timid person or a coward is very far from steadiness of mind.

21

Thus, always keeping the mind balanced, the yogi, with the mind controlled, attains the peace abiding in Me, which culminates in liberation. (6:15)

The Supreme Self is an embodiment of peace. It is an ocean of peace. When one attains the supreme peace of samatvam, by controlling the modifications of the mind and keeping it always balanced, one attains liberation or perfection.

Little by little let him attain quietude by holding the intellect firmly; having made the mind establish itself in the Self, let him not think of anything. (6:25)

The practitioner of yoga should attain tranquillity gradually, by degrees, by means of the intellect controlled by steadiness. The peace of the Eternal will fill the heart gradually with bliss through constant and protracted practice of steady concentration. He should make the mind constantly abide in the Self within through ceaseless practice. If one constantly thinks of the immortal Self within, the mind will cease to think of objects of sensual pleasure. The mental energy should be directed along the spiritual channel by *atma chintan* or constant contemplation of the Self.

From whatever cause the restless and unsteady mind wanders away, from that let him restrain it and bring it under the control of the Self alone. (6:26)

In this verse the Lord gives the method to control and steady the mind. You will have to drag the mind to your point of centre again and again when it runs towards external objects. If you make the mind taste the eternal bliss of the Self within, little by little, by the practice of concentration, it will gradually abide in the Self only and not run towards external sense objects. Sound and other objects only make the mind restless and unsteady. By knowing the defects of objects of sensual pleasure, by understanding their illusory nature, by cultivating discrimination between the real and the unreal and also by dispassion, and by making the mind understand the glory and the splendour of the Self, you can wean the mind entirely away from sensual objects and fix it firmly on the Self.

> Supreme bliss verily comes to this yogi whose mind is quite peaceful, whose passion is quieted, who has become Brahman and who is free from impurities. (6:27)

Eternal, unalloyed and uninterrupted bliss comes to the yogi whose mind is perfectly serene, who has calmed his passionate nature, who has destroyed all sorts of attachments, who has attained knowledge of the Self, thus becoming a *jivanmukta*, one who is liberated while living, who feels that all is Brahman only, and who is taintless, unaffected by *dharma* or *adharma*, righteousness and unrighteousness.

> With the mind harmonized by yoga, he sees the Self abiding in all beings and all beings in the Self; he sees the same everywhere. (6: 29)

The yogi beholds through the eye of intuition the oneness or unity of the Self everywhere. This is a sublime and magnanimous vision indeed. He feels, "All indeed is Brahman." He beholds that all beings are one with Brahman and that the Self and Brahman are identical.

> He who is the same to foe and friend, and also in honour and dishonour, who is the same in cold and heat and in pleasure and pain, who is free from attachment, to whom censure and praise are equal, who is silent, content with anything, homeless, of a steady mind, and full of devotion – that person is very dear to Me. (12:18–19)

The ordinary man of the world is ruled by duality, by the pairs of opposites, but a yogi or a sage has a balanced mind. He has poise or equanimity. He is not swayed by the blind forces of attraction and repulsion. He has no attachment for objects of any kind. He has controlled the organ of speech and so he is silent. His mind is also serene and silent as he has controlled the thoughts. He is quite content with the bare means of bodily sustenance. He has no fixed abode. He regards the world as his dwelling place. His mind is ever fixed on Brahman.

This is the description of a rare yogi who has attained samatvam, equanimity of mind. He is regarded as the highest among yogis. He has dissolved all duality in the underlying unity and thus sees the Self of all in all beings, from Brahman the creator down to a blade of grass. He sees that whatever is pleasure or pain for himself is also pleasure or pain for all other beings. He does not harm anyone. He wishes good to all. He is compassionate to all creatures. He has a very soft and large heart. Established in the unity of the Self, he beholds the Self everywhere, and thus sees equality everywhere.

Pain and pleasure have no meaning to this sage who dwells in his own Self. He is above the pairs of opposites. In his eyes cow dung or gold, a jewel or a stone, are of equal value. He is free from the idea of giving and taking. His mind is not perturbed by anything, pleasant or unpleasant. He is the same towards agreeable and disagreeable things. Praise and censure cannot affect him. He stands adamant. Wherever he lives, he abides in his own essential state as Existence-Knowledge-Bliss Absolute. He is ever calm and serene. He is the yoga of equanimity personified!

Read these words of Lord Krishna's over and over again. Sincere aspirants, always hold before yourselves this portrait of the yogi who has attained the highest virtue. Make every effort to practise the yoga of equanimity. Free yourself from worldly ignorance in order that you may experience the supreme spiritual peace of samatvam and attain the highest vision of the Absolute. May God bless all with peace and prosperity!

3

The Pathway to Samatvam

An aspirant who treads the path of samatvam must make every effort to acquire the following essential qualities: discrimination, *viveka*, dispassion, *vairagya*, the six virtues, *shadsampat*, and an intense desire for liberation, *mumukshutva*. In order to possess the virtue of samatvam, he will also need to dedicate himself to steadying the mind every moment of his yoga career, because if the mind is restless, not an iota of progress can be made in the attainment of this divine quality. All over the world there are peace conferences, peace talks and peace walks. They are no doubt laudable and beneficial, but unless we all consciously strive for equanimity through meditation, prayer and other spiritual practices, no one in this world will be able to achieve true, everlasting peace of mind. To attain the state of samatvam the aspirant will have to prepare himself while living amongst all the ups and downs of life.

How can this preparation be made? Carefully study the words of Lord Krishna in the *Bhagavad Gita*. In this magnificent dialogue between Lord Krishna and his disciple, Arjuna, all the qualities of one who has attained the yoga of equanimity are given. In that description the Lord also tells Arjuna the sadhana that leads to the yoga of equanimity, samatvam.

The pathway to samatvam yoga is a combination of four spiritual disciplines. One component is self-knowledge or self-enquiry, acquired through jnana yoga. Another part lies in the way of action, karma yoga. The aspirant then requires the qualities of self-restraint or control of the mind, which can be attained through the practices of raja yoga. Jnana yoga removes the veil of ignorance and brings knowledge of the Self. Raja yoga steadies the mind. Karma yoga removes the tossing of the mind. Through bhakti yoga the aspirant adds faith and devotion. Faith and devotion will unite jnana, raja and karma yogas. However, in the final analysis, the yogi of equanimity and steady wisdom must attribute all his actions to the Divine, Ishwara or God. Therefore, faith is the divine ingredient required for the yoga of equanimity. Only with unflinching faith and sincere devotion to sadhana can an aspirant overcome all the obstacles on this difficult path.

The pathway to samatvam harmonizes wonderfully the philosophy of self-knowledge, action and devotion. One will need the head of Adi Shankaracharya, the hands of King Janaka and the heart of Lord Buddha. The three horses of this body-chariot, intellect, action and emotion, should work in perfect harmony. Only then will it move smoothly and reach its destination. Learn the methods from jnana yoga and raja yoga to subdue the senses and the mind, and to practice concentration, meditation and know the Self. Try to experience oneness with the divine power by directing the mind to the Lord. Develop intense faith. Practise bhakti yoga. Learn to surrender to the will of God. Understand and practice the technique of selfless service or karma yoga and renunciation of the fruits of actions.

The Lord enunciates the pathway to samatvam when he tells Arjuna in the *Bhagavad Gita*:

> One who is full of faith, who is devoted to it, and who has subdued the senses obtains this knowledge; and, having obtained the knowledge he goes at once to the supreme peace. (4:39)

Following this pathway is certain to culminate in the yoga of equanimity. All three qualifications of self-knowledge, faith and selfless service are indispensable for every aspirant treading this path. One alone will not suffice. Only by perfecting all these qualities can the aspirant rejoice in the highest peace within. Acquire the qualities of dispassion and discrimination, obtain the wisdom of the sixfold virtues, and attain the highest knowledge through introspection, concentration and meditation. One will also need to excel as a karma yogi, and, most importantly, have the yearning to become a yogi of the highest class. Samatvam yoga is not an easy process, but it will take the aspirant to the uppermost rung of spiritual life.

4

Discrimination and Dispassion

DISCRIMINATION

The first essential requisite for acquiring an equipoised mind is *viveka*, discrimination between the real and the unreal. One in whom right reason has developed will be able to discriminate and enjoy peace and bliss. Sensual pleasure is tantalizing and excites the mind. Most people are swayed by emotions, passions and impulses and thus run wildly after every object they come in contact with. Their minds become full of anxieties and they become despondent as to whether or not their desired objects will be secured. The moment they possess the objects, they find the satisfaction of the senses lasts for a few seconds only, and they must then seek for pleasures elsewhere to give them some peace of mind. Knowing no way out of this vicious cycle, they remain entangled in their search for pleasure. Their lives are constantly mixed with pain and anxiety from fear of losing the pleasurable objects. Wherever there is pleasure, pain, then anger and attachment will be found.

Dear aspirant, awaken from your hallucinations. Seek peace of mind! Owing to delusion, pain appears as pleasure, and the fear of pain worries you. There is no pleasure or pain for a discriminating mind. Learn to discriminate between the real and the unreal. The yoga of equanimity can be had only by one who has understood the worthlessness of perishable objects. The world is nothing to a *viveki*, a man of discrimination. He never becomes entangled in anything. Discrimination gives inner strength and mental peace.

One who has found out the real worth of this world, who yearns for liberation, who has understood that beyond the names and forms there is one eternal, everlasting Atman, and who practises self-discipline, he alone can have peace. Such a person is the king of kings, not he who is simply carried away by a little colour, by a touch and a little titillation. He who does not discriminate between the eternal and the non-eternal, between the real and the unreal, is forever miserable with an unsteady, passionate mind.

Whenever a desire arises in the mind, always consult your power of discrimination. It will at once tell you that the desire is attended with pain, that it is only a vain temptation set up by the mind and that discrimination alone can bring about satisfaction and peace of mind. It will advise you to renounce the desire immediately and take up study of the Upanishads, repetition of Om and reach for samadhi. Desires will become extinct with the rise of discrimination. When desires cease, the mind becomes silent and stands still in perfect equipoise.

A sincere aspirant must make every effort to control desires the moment they arise. Think deeply again and again whether the new desire will give more happiness or more spiritual gain. Viveka will guide you to call on your willpower and drive away the desire immediately. On the path of samatvam, discrimination and willpower are two potent weapons to help destroy temptations, and remove major and minor impediments.

When a desire arises in the mind, a worldling welcomes it and tries to fulfil it, but a sincere aspirant renounces it immediately through discrimination. Wise men consider even a spark of desire to be a great evil. They remain ever delighted in the Atman only. Their mind becomes steady. Every action is poised and harmonious.

DISPASSION

From *viveka,* discrimination, is born *vairagya,* dispassion or non-attachment, the second spiritual requisite for attaining even-mindedness. It is the mind that links man with the body, and when man identifies with the body, all his miseries begin. He thinks of 'I'-ness and 'mine'-ness, which are the two poisonous fangs of the mind-serpent. If these two fangs are extracted, the serpent-mind will be tamed and then there can be no bondage. Those who practise non-attachment are the real tamers of their minds. Vairagya thins out the mind, acting as a drastic purgative. Non-attachment is indifference or dispassion towards sensual objects. Attachment to objects is universal, and no one is free from attachment of one kind or another. Attachment is the first child of *maya,* illusion, and her most powerful weapon, binding one to the endless wheel of birth and death.

Attachment is the root cause of all human suffering, the product of ignorance. The seeds of attachment are ingrained in the subconscious mind, and have to be obliterated through right thinking, enquiry and spiritual knowledge. All these illusory attachments have to be cut asunder with the sword of non-attachment. Wherever there is strong attachment, infatuation and fear will be found. The cause of fear is attachment to this body and property. Attachment and fear destroy balance of mind and cause the emotions to swing wildly. When one is free from attachment to external objects, the mind will be at peace.

The whole divine play of the Lord is kept up by the force of attachment to worldly life. Greed for possessions generates selfishness, which causes even greater attachment. However, the type of renunciation advocated on the pathway to samatvam does not require one to renounce family life. Balance of mind has to be attained while living in the world, learning through the world without becoming enmeshed in it. Your duty is to maintain your household without getting attached to it. Only then will you have the purity of mind which will enable you to progress towards perennial peace.

The activities of daily life do not bring misery; it is attachment and identification with people, places and events that brings all sorts of worries, troubles and unhappiness. Work without attachment or identification. This attitude is the secret of success in karma yoga or selfless service. Only then can one have real happiness and peace of mind, and attain God-consciousness. This is *jnana*, the fire of wisdom which burns all the fruits of actions. Discipline the mind carefully. When old habits creep in, destroy them at the very root. Lead a life of perfect non-attachment. This is the master key with which to open the realms of serenity of mind and eternal bliss.

The mind wreaks havoc and mischief. One may still rule a vast dominion and yet be unattached. Look at the exalted mental state of King Janaka, who was resting in his own essential divine nature. He said, "Even if the whole of Mithila is burnt, nothing of mine will be burnt." He had not the least attachment to his wealth and kingdom. The mind has to be trained daily in all its dealings and actions. Do not become attached to family and property. The world is like a public inn. People are united for some time and separated after some time. Never say, "My body, my son, my wife, my house."

Attachment takes various forms. Always be on the alert to detect its subtle workings. The mind tries its utmost to become attached to some form or other. Its nature is to leave one form and immediately cling to another. If the binding link in the mind is destroyed, one can roam about peacefully in any part of the world, unattached, like water on a lotus leaf. Nothing can bind you then.

Dispassion is a mental state. Inner spiritual strength is born of dispassion. Develop intense internal dispassion by understanding the illusory nature of this world. Turn the mind towards God and practise daily mantra japa and meditation. Read the lives of great saints and yogis and books on atma jnana, meditation and the service of humanity.

31

Take recourse to the company of saints and devotees. Study Vedanta and Bhartrihari's *Vairagya Shatakam*. Lead a life of non-attachment to this world. Vairagya is real spiritual wealth because it opens the door to equanimity, everlasting peace and bliss.

> Undoubtedly, O mighty-armed Arjuna, the mind is difficult to control and restless, but by practice and by dispassion it may be restrained. (6:35)

These are the words of Lord Krishna in the *Bhagavad Gita*. He recognizes that to work without attachment is doubtless a difficult task, but it becomes possible for an aspirant with the patience and determination to succeed in samatvam sadhana.

5

The Sixfold Virtues

The sixfold virtues, known as *shadsampat*, are: *shama*, mental calmness and control, *dama*, restraint of the senses, *uparati*, sense withdrawal or pratyahara, *titiksha*, endurance, *shraddha*, faith, and *samadhana*, mental balance. They are taken as one because they are calculated to bring about mental control and discipline. These six virtues are the third requisite for attaining samatvam.

To attain samatvam, one must constantly struggle to purify and steady the mind. Armed with the sixfold virtues the aspirant can be successful in stopping the fluctuations of the mind and eventually control it. If the mind is purged of its impurities and worldly taints, it will become exceedingly calm, free from differentiations such as 'I', 'you' and 'he'. All tribulations, annoyances and miseries will cease and then worldly delusion, attendant with its births and deaths, will come to an end, and one will attain the supreme abode of peace.

On one side of the mind is matter and on the other side is the serenity of pure spirit, *atman*. The mind forms a bridge between the two. Cross the bridge by controlling the mind. Attain samatvam by utilizing the wisdom of the sixfold virtues.

1. SHAMA: CALMNESS OF MIND

Shama, calmness and tranquillity of mind, is most difficult to achieve, even for the most advanced yogi. However, with practice and dispassion the mind will become calm as time goes by and gradually come under control. To attain samatvam, an aspirant must remain cool and serene, even in the most provocative conditions and circumstances. Shama must be cultivated again and again through constant endeavour. Serenity is like a rock. Waves of irritation may dash on it but cannot affect it. A serene mind is a valuable spiritual asset, and for this the world is a wonderful training ground. The divine light will descend only on a calm mind.

Desire is the enemy of peace. Give up the feeling of 'I-ness' and 'mineness', name and fame. Possessiveness strengthens the ego. Try not to fulfil your desires or expect anything. Overcome vicious desires by developing virtuous desires and then destroy them by having one strong desire for steadiness of mind. Peace is in the heart of a desireless person who has controlled the senses and the mind.

Practising the yamas and niyamas as expounded in Maharishi Patanjali's *Yoga Sutras* will help to check all the desires, eliminate mental impurities and attain mastery over the mind. The mind will become quiet. Pranayama destroys rajas and tamas, making the mind steady and one-pointed. Once mental dissipation vanishes, the mind becomes balanced and very, very calm. The peace that you will enjoy cannot be adequately described.

If you are easily carried away by surging emotions and impulses, if you are in the grip of moods, cravings and passions, if you laugh for five minutes and weep for five hours, how can you claim the yoga of equanimity? In this Kali Yuga the easiest way to control the mind and emotions and attain serenity is kirtan or singing the name of the Lord. Sattwic qualities of mind like sympathy, compassion, universal love, forgiveness and spiritual patience should be cultivated to a very high degree. Bad habits can be eradicated by establishing new good habits. The lower instinctive mind has to be controlled by the higher sattwic mind. Moderating the diet and taking sattwic foods will calm the mind, whereas rajasic foods will excite the mind.

Learn to control the mind so that the thoughts may always be calm and unruffled. Sit alone and watch the wanderings of the mind. Remain as a witness and do not identify with the thoughts that come and go. The mind will gradually come under your control. By destroying the fuel of desire, the fire of thought will be extinguished. Do not compare yourself with others. Do not think of the past. Do not plan for the future. Do not allow the mind to build images. Live in the solid present. This allows the mind to become calm and still.

Counter-thoughts

Pratipaksha bhavana, the method of substituting an opposite thought or counter-thought, enables one to lead a happy, harmonious life of peace and power. A thought of love will at once neutralize a thought of hatred. A thought of courage will immediately serve as a powerful antidote against a thought of fear. Ideas create the world. Ideas develop the desires and excite the passions. So a contrary idea of destroying desires and passions will counteract the former idea of satisfying them.

When there is irritability, meditate on the virtues of tolerance and self-restraint. If depressed, fill the mind with the idea of joy and exhilaration. When sick, fill the mind with ideas of health, strength and vitality. This is a great sadhana. Worldly thoughts, thoughts of enmity, hatred, revenge and anger will all die. Do not cause pain or suffering to any living being due to greed, selfishness, irritability or annoyance. For an aspirant who is leading the divine life and aspiring to samatvam, this is a very serious drawback.

Control anger by meditating on patience. Give up arguing and heated debates which upset one's balance of mind. When a wave of anger arises in the mind, stand as a witness and identify with the Self. Practise self-analysis and introspection. Ask: "Who am I?" "What do I gain by becoming angry? The self is an embodiment of peace." When you enquire and reflect in this manner, the wave of anger will die by itself. By striving and making a sincere effort to subdue your anger, hatred will also cease. Do not express anger, but try to control it. Cut short its duration by turning the mind to japa, singing kirtan, or any other pleasant and inspiring occupation. One who has controlled anger acts with equipoise.

Control of speech

Controlling the speech has to be practised to attain quick progress in the yoga of equanimity. Four attributes need to be combined: one's words must be non-exciting and non-painful, truthful, pleasant and beneficial at the same time. Avoid impulsive, emotional utterances and boisterous expressions. The organ of speech is a restless sense, so think before you speak. The words of a person who practises speech control bring cheer and solace to others. Perfect control over speech means control of the mind. Otherwise thoughtless words will disturb your mind and the minds of the others.

Speak the truth at any cost, in a way that is not calculated to hurt the feelings of others. Know the power of each word uttered and the effect it will produce on the minds of others. Observing *mouna,* measured speech, for a couple of hours daily will develop willpower and remove anxieties. A new type of inner peace will then be experienced. One who weighs his words before expressing them will have great peace of mind. Lord Jesus was a sage who measured words in his speech. Mahatma Gandhi was also a man of measured speech. A talkative person cannot dream of having peace of mind even for a short time. Control of speech conserves energy and gives peace of mind and inner strength.

It is very, very difficult to understand another person's mind, even someone you have known closely for years. It is also very difficult to understand one's own mind. If you really want to eradicate the unbalancing habits and traits of your character, you will have to be in close contact with a developed yogi or with your guru for some years. You cannot detect your own defects. Those who have freed themselves from the fluctuation of their minds come into possession of supreme calmness. One who has controlled his mind is a true hero. When the mind is purged of all its impurities, it will become very calm and worldly delusions will soon be eradicated. That is peace of mind.

2. DAMA: RESTRAINT OF THE SENSES

Dama is mental control of the senses. The senses can be subdued through the constant practice of self-restraint. Freed from all kinds of sensual cravings, likes and dislikes, attraction and repulsion, one can possess evenness of mind. Only those who have stilled the mind are neither elated nor troubled when they get desirable or undesirable objects. For a sincere aspirant, discipline of the senses is a very important sadhana. Such an aspirant needs to watch every sense carefully and curb it through suitable methods such as fasting, observing silence, trataka, celibacy, renouncing sense objects, observing self-restraint and pratyahara. Curbing the senses means curbing the mind. The senses cannot work independently without the direct help of the mind.

Through introspection find out which sense is troubling you and curb it carefully. Give up the objects which that particular sense tries to grasp. Overcome craving by taking only what is necessary for healthy survival. Then you will be established in supreme peace. Many aspirants fail to attain samatvam due to the restlessness of a particular sense organ.

Observing silence controls the organ of speech. Practising trataka, gazing at a point, will help to control the eyes. When the eyes run towards objects of beauty, withdraw them and fix them at the lotus feet of Lord Krishna. When the ears run to listen to worldly sounds and music, train them to hear the name 'Narayana'. Giving up salt and sugar for a week and living on simple food will help to control the tongue, the organ of taste. Sleeping on a hard mat and walking bare-footed helps to discipline the skin, the organ of touch.

Fix the mind on your ishta devata. Bring it back again and again when it wanders and fix it on the image. This is the sadhana for checking the wandering mind and developing concentration. By constant, regular practice, one can steadily fix the mind on God. One who has disciplined the senses has a strong will and peace of mind. Higher spiritual sadhana is not possible without restraint of the senses.

Discrimination

To understand the significance of self-restraint, a more comprehensive view of the senses must be taken. Human beings are given these senses together with the superior faculty of discrimination, and the senses must operate under its wise supervision. The ultimate aim of self-restraint is not denial of the senses, but the achievement of a state of existence a millionfold greater than the experience of sense gratification. For the spiritual aspirant, self-restraint is not a matter of repression, but a joyous, voluntary discipline undertaken for the acquisition of a perfectly balanced and steady mind. That is the highest view that the sages uphold for spiritual aspirants.

Yoga recommends appropriate restraint of the senses to achieve the yoga of equanimity and their proper utilization for the welfare of all God's creation. The tongue can repeat the guru stotras; the ears can hear the shrutis and other spiritual texts. The unlimited potentialities of the senses are to be harnessed for the greater good. Viewed from this angle, the aspirant is asked not to starve and destroy the mind and senses, but really to strengthen them and utilize them for his own spiritual evolution. Ultimately, the senses are to be consecrated at the feet of the Lord for His service alone.

Those who are content with whatever comes their way have strong minds and tremendous self-restraint. A contented mind is a very great virtue. It is one of the four sentinels of the vast domain of *moksha*, liberation. If you have this virtue, it will lead to the attainment of equipoise.

Take everything as it comes, instead of complaining. Seize every opportunity. In this way a great deal of mental strength and evenness of mind is gained and the power of endurance and patience is developed. Make use of outer disturbances and noise for the practice of concentration. Develop the power to remain undisturbed no matter what happens. This power comes with practice. Learning to work under changing conditions means progress, and a great deal of mental control.

The practice of contentment is a sattwic virtue that propels the aspirant towards God. It gives strength of mind and peace, checks unnecessary and selfish exertions, opens the inner eye and moves the mind towards divine contemplation. A contented person is always peaceful, more energetic, introspective and of steady mind. He recognizes the inner life of the atman within. He turns out more work calmly and with a one-pointed mind. Contentment emboldens an aspirant to march fearlessly along the rugged and thorny path of samatvam.

Moderation

In the *Bhagavad Gita*, Lord Krishna prescribes this path of moderation:

> "Yoga becomes the destroyer of pain for one who is moderate in eating and recreation (such as walking, etc.), who is moderate in exertion in actions, who is moderate in sleep and wakefulness" (6:17)

Moderation is really self-restraint. Moderation is equanimity, it is skill in yoga. Be moderate in eating, drinking, sleeping, reading, laughing, talking and exercise. Overeating causes drowsiness and overtaxes the internal organs. Too much sleep makes one dull and lazy. Too much sexual activity drains the energy. Too much talking disturbs one's peace of mind and causes exhaustion. If one overworks, one cannot concentrate. Sadhana also needs to be well regulated and suited to one's temperament.

What is needed is strong mental dispassion born of strong discrimination. Have intense dispassion internally and at the same time follow the middle path externally. Do not unbalance the mind or spoil the body in the name of austerities. Balance of mind cannot be attained by going to extremes. Only when Lord Buddha gave up extreme austerities and regulated his spiritual practices did he attain illumination. Therefore, to attain equanimity of mind lead a well regulated and disciplined life and be moderate in everything, then composure can be maintained at all times.

3. UPARATI: SENSE WITHDRAWAL

Uparati is the turning away of the mind from objects of sensual desire and enjoyment. It is the state of mind which is always engaged inwardly, without being diverted, and it comes naturally when one has grasped viveka, vairagya, shama and dama. By perfecting pratyahara, one will attain the state of uparati and gain great control over the mind.

Pratyahara is withdrawal of the senses from sense objects. The practice of pratyahara puts a break or a check on the senses. Regular practice will stop the outgoing tendencies of the senses. The outgoing senses will have to be dragged away from sensual objects and the mind fixed on one's point of concentration. Learn to drag the senses gently. Practise withdrawal of the senses one by one. Deal with the most turbulent sense first, and then take up another sense organ. Trying to manipulate all the senses at the same time will not lead to success. If the aspirant is not careful, if his dispassion wanes, and if he is not regular in his sadhana, a reaction sets in, the senses become more turbulent and control becomes very difficult.

Dispassion and renunciation help in the practice of pratyahara. If one succeeds in this practice, concentration comes by itself. If you can consciously practise pratyahara at will by deliberately attaching and detaching the mind to and from the senses, you have really gained great control over the mind and can then check the outgoing tendencies of the mind at any time.

Generally, people jump to the practice of concentration without practising pratyahara in the beginning. That is the reason why they fail in concentration, and then cannot proceed to meditation practices. However, one who has succeeded in pratyahara can concentrate the mind quite readily for a very long time. Pratyahara is a very important state of mind. It is the stepping stone to *samatvam*, equipoise of mind.

4. TITIKSHA: ENDURANCE

Titiksha, or the power of endurance, develops the willpower. The ability to face difficulties with calm endurance in pleasure and pain, heat and cold, is one of the most essential qualifications for an aspirant on the path of samatvam. Do not lose heart in adverse circumstances, but endure them with a smiling countenance. Become a real warrior and conquer the enemies within the mind, the senses, desires, impressions and cravings, those forces which have robbed you of your atmic jewel of equipoise. The spiritual battlefield demands greater valour, patience, perseverance, strength, courage and skill than the battlefield in the outer world. Every difficulty that comes is an opportunity to grow stronger and to develop the will. When you have decided to take to the spiritual path, stick to it at any cost, come what may.

Do not murmur or grumble when troubles and sorrows descend, but endure them. Difficulties strengthen the will, augment the power of endurance and turn the mind towards God. Face them with a smile. In your weakness lies your real strength. Nothing can harm you. You are invincible. Conquer difficulties one by one. Endurance is one of the divine qualities that Lord Krishna explained to Arjuna in simple terms in the *Bhagavad Gita*:

The contact of the senses with objects which cause sensations of heat and cold, pleasure and pain, have a

41

beginning and an end; they are impermanent. Endure them bravely, O Arjuna. The firm man who is not afflicted by these, who is balanced in pleasure and pain, is fit to attain immortality. (2:14–15)

Titiksha by itself cannot give equanimity, but when coupled with discrimination, dispassion and faith, it becomes a means to attain steady wisdom. The one thought, "I am the immortal Self," will infuse courage and inner spiritual strength, and enable you to endure everything. Cultivate endurance, right thought and right action. Thinking that you are the immortal Self is right thinking. Working unselfishly and dispassionately, with the feeling that you are serving the Lord in all, that all your actions are worship of Him, is right action.

Exert. Practise endurance. Concentrate. Purify. Meditate. Do not become a fatalist. Do not yield to inertia. Do not bleat like a lamb. Roar, "*Om, Om, Om,*" like a lion of Vedanta. If the power of endurance is developed, if one thinks that everything is done by God for one's own betterment, if painful events are viewed as messengers from God to make one remember Him and to infuse more mercy and the power of endurance, suffering will not be suffering any more. Only with this divine outlook on life will constant, perpetual serenity of mind be enjoyed, even amidst great turmoil and calamities.

Have a new angle of vision. You will see no necessity for selfish worldly struggles to accumulate wealth, no need of name and fame. Greed, hatred and turmoil will then disappear completely. You will be free from all pain and torment. This is not only the philosophy of the stoics or the teaching of the pessimists. It is a condition of right knowledge. It is wonderful optimism that goads the aspirant on to realize the deep, abiding eternal joy and unruffled peace of the Self within.

Remember that you are the master of your destiny. You can also work wonders and miracles if you apply yourself to spiritual sadhana. Surely success in the yoga of samatvam is bound to manifest if you decide to endure everything that arises in your spiritual quest. Have full trust and confidence in the Divine. *Tat Twam Asi* – 'Thou Art That'.

5. SHRADDHA: FAITH

Shraddha is faith. Faith is the greatest thing in the world. Not an iota of progress is ever possible on the spiritual path without faith. If one has no faith in the world, the world does not exist. If there is no faith in sensual objects, they will not give pleasure. Man lives and is guided by faith. Whatever a person strongly believes in he experiences and becomes. Those who have no faith in God do not know what is right and wrong; they lose their power of discrimination. When faith is directed to God, it becomes the cause of liberation.

Faith in God is the first step towards samatvam. This path is fraught with struggles against the senses and the temptations and desires that arise in the mind. Discrimination, complete dispassion for mundane things, self-restraint, tranquillity of mind and a strong yearning for liberation are the prerequisites for attaining samatvam. Divine wisdom and expert guidance are required to purify the heart, to become simple and straightforward. Therefore, every aspirant on the path of samatvam must possess faith as his fundamental virtue. The faith must be a living faith, unflinching and unshakeable, if the aspirant is to overcome the forces of delusion that surround him.

Whenever doubts assail you, reject them ruthlessly. Abandon all sorts of wrong beliefs, superstitions, weaknesses, wrong notions and ideas of impossibilities. Cling fast to faith in divine possibilities. Have faith in divine life. Faith is omnipotent. Always feel the help of the invisible hands of God during worldly activities. The Lord is always with you, watching all your activities and thoughts. Aspire fervently and constantly to live in the Divine. The voice of the mind will delude you, but the voice of the soul will uplift you and take you to the goal. Only by placing implicit faith in the existence of God, in the teachings of one's guru, in the Vedas and in one's own self can one successfully tread this path of samatvam.

The path to samatvam is difficult, and therefore you will need the guidance of the great gurus who have walked the path successfully. Search for your guru with faith, and then approach that sage in a spirit of humility and devotion. His help, personal example, encouragement and grace are needed to attain success in sadhana. One who reverentially seeks the guidance of a guru will be blessed. The mind cannot but recognize the silence and stillness in the company of divine people.

If God so wished, He could give equanimity to every single person in the world in an instant, but this form of God's grace will descend only on those who prepare themselves to receive it. His grace descends in proportion to the degree of the devotee's surrender; the more the surrender, the more the grace. So, dear aspirant, be up and doing! Persevere! Only then will the Lord shower His grace of serenity upon you.

God will lift us out of the ocean of worldly existence if we fix our minds on Him unswervingly with devotion and worship Him with undivided attention. Remembrance of God at all times continuously is a very difficult sadhana, yet the most potent and the surest way of attaining equanimity. The mind is maya; it deludes and misleads. Pain appears as pleasure. The mind charged with attraction, repulsion, anger and jealousy is a blazing furnace. Faith in God is the only way to free oneself from birth, death, old age, disease and grief, from care, worry, anxiety, fear and disappointment. Worldly powers of fame, name and fortune will never give everlasting happiness.

Feel that the Lord's supreme power does everything. We are all His instruments. Whosoever surrenders his selfish aims and interests to the will of the Lord will enjoy supreme peace and perennial bliss. Let the hands be ever engaged in service of the Lord. Let the mind be ever thinking of His glories. Let the intellect discriminate correctly. Then the soul will be ever in peaceful union with the Lord.

6. SAMADHANA

Samadhana refers to mental balance and self-settledness of mind. It is the fruit of the practice of shama, dama, uparati, titiksha and shraddha. Samadhana is fixing the mind on the atman, and not allowing it to run towards sense objects. When the mind wanders from contemplation to a worldly object and finds it worthless, it returns to its object of contemplation and tries to stay there, as it is satisfied with the Self. This is samadhana.

Samadhana is the state of mind which is free from anxiety amidst difficulties and indifferent among pleasure. Such an aspirant is quite indifferent to the world as he is very much attracted to the Self. Without union with the Self, neither harmony nor balance nor samadhi is possible. If the mind tastes the eternal bliss of the Self within, little by little, by the practice of concentration, it will gradually abide in the Self only and not run towards external sense objects.

Samadhana is a refined state of mind. Ignorance, *avidya,* which is the cause of exhilaration, grief and bondage to worldly existence, will need to be destroyed through knowledge of the Self. By understanding the illusory nature of objects of sensual pleasure, by cultivating discrimination between the real and the unreal and also by dispassion, and by making the mind understand the glory and splendour of the Self, the mind can be weaned away entirely from sensual pleasure and fixed firmly on the Self. Develop dispassion, patience and perseverance to the maximum. Have unshakeable faith in the existence of God and in the efficacy of spiritual practices. Such a goal requires strong determination and the power of endurance.

Samadhana is an accomplishment gained over several lives from prolonged sadhana. One who experiences the state of samadhana can almost savour the peace of samatvam yoga. In the *Bhagavad Gita*, Lord Krishna describes the perfectly controlled mind, the mind with self-settledness:

> When the perfectly controlled mind rests in the Self only, free from longing for all the objects of desires, then it is said, 'He is united, harmonized or balanced'. (6:18)

Tame the five-hooded serpent

A steady mind is not a commodity that can be purchased in the market. It is a rare, hidden treasure guarded by a five-hooded serpent. Unless this serpent is tamed, one cannot have access to that treasure. That treasure is the yoga of equanimity, samatvam, which is the spiritual wealth of a perfectly balanced mind.

The serpent is the mind. The five hoods are the senses through which the mind-serpent hisses. Discipline and purification of the mind and the senses are prerequisites for an aspirant on the path of samatvam. If you are able to curb egoism and selfishness, if you are not swayed by likes and dislikes, if you have equal vision, a broad heart and an open mind, if you possess a sterling character and good manners under all circumstances, if you value the need of others above your own, and if your mind is ever engaged in contemplation of His all-pervading presence, then you can assure yourself that you are definitely on the path of samatvam.

Unless the mind is tamed so that one can cast off all desires, cravings, worries, delusion, pride, attachment, likes and dislikes, it cannot enter into the domain of supreme peace and unalloyed felicity of the immortal abode. There is no other vessel on this earth on which one can cross the ocean of samsara other than mastery of the antagonistic mind. Only those who have controlled the serpent of the mind will reach the realm of equanimity.

The aspirant who is full of faith and devotion and has subdued the senses surely realizes transcendental knowledge and attains the yoga of equanimity. In that ultimate state of peace all pains are extinguished. The aspirant will be released from bondage to actions. He will become immortal and obtain divine wisdom. His mind will be calm and remain ever balanced. He will neither rejoice on obtaining what is pleasant, nor feel sorry on obtaining what is unpleasant. He will have happiness beyond the reach of the senses. When established in samatvam yoga, the yoga of equanimity, he will not be shaken even by heavy sorrow. He will be ever established in divine consciousness. He will become one with God and attain eternal, infinite, unbroken bliss. Through His grace may you attain supreme bliss, supreme peace and supreme knowledge.

6

Mumukshutva

Mumukshutva is intense longing for liberation. An equipoised mind is hard to attain, but success comes to those who dare and act; it seldom comes to the timid. Sincere, intense longing is essential. Spiritual life is a continuous struggle against one's own lower nature. Yet, when purified, the lower self feels a mighty urge for expansion into its essential nature of absolute serenity and silence.

Realize more and more your true, essential, peaceful nature. The more you yearn to turn over a new leaf and lead a pure, divine life, the more opportunities will come. Have one all-consuming aspiration. Pray to the Lord from the bottom of your heart. Attain inner peace and live in inner peace. Keep your godward aspiration ever alive.

Every aspirant must develop a fervent desire for God, as this one strong desire to attain self-realization will destroy all the other worldly desires. The strength of one's longing should be the invincible strength born of wisdom and discrimination between the real and the unreal, born of one's sincerity and whole-hearted dedication to the yoga of equanimity. Be prepared to sacrifice everything. How then can one fail to attain the highest state of tranquillity? How then can the aspirant fail to become the highest yogi? Spiritual yearning must be real and lasting. Only then can one have spiritual progress and be able to stick to the path.

A life of sadhana must become a passion, so be firm in your vows and fiery in your determination. Every failure is a movement towards success. Every difficulty or disappointment is a trial of your faith. Be a hero and win the spiritual battle. Spiritual sadhana is uphill work and requires tremendous patience and perseverance. The mind is now annoyed and now quiet. Never yield to it. Be serene, balanced and steady. Overcome whatever obstacles come in the way through self-effort, faith and surrender. Adaptability and an iron will can turn all obstacles into stepping stones.

Be a light unto yourself. Calmly bear insults, privations and sufferings. Be harmonious everywhere, with everybody. Act nobly, live peacefully, endure pain. There is nothing comparable with peace in this world. Therefore, carry on your spiritual practices with unabated zeal, and you are bound to succeed. Blessed is the earnest aspirant who possesses an adamantine will to attain spiritual virtues.

7

Introspection and Contemplation

One who practises daily introspection and self-analysis can discover his defects and habits and remove them. This is very patient work. Through introspection, an aspirant gains knowledge of the laws and ways of the mind and can easily check its wanderings and manage it perfectly. During introspection, the rapid shifting of the mind from one line of thought to another can be clearly observed.

Herein lies a chance to mould the mind properly and direct the thoughts and mental energy into the divine channel. Throw out worldly and useless thoughts, and do not allow the intruders of anger, greed, delusion and pride to enter the mental factory. This is a stupendous task indeed, but success is sure with daily introspection. The practice demands patience, perseverance, tenacity, iron will, a subtle intellect and courage. Concentration can be practised uninterruptedly. The reward is invaluable. It is immortality, supreme peace and infinite bliss.

Find peace in the Self
Man is essentially a spiritual being expressing himself through the mind and body. His innermost essence is the *atma* or divine spirit. Man is not this body, not his senses or even his mind; these are only his vehicles. The body and mind are subject to change, decay and death, whereas the real man, the immortal Self, is never-ending and eternal.

Only a calm mind can grasp the Truth, see the immortal Self and receive the divine light.

The mind has the power to reflect, to look into its own depths. An aspirant must learn the art of making the mind introspective or turned inward upon itself. If you go above body consciousness and if the mind rests in the Self, then you are happy, peaceful and free. Acquire the power of introspection. A raja yogi develops this power through self-enquiry. When, by analyzing your own mind, you come face to face with something which is by its own nature eternally pure, perfect, self-luminous and unchanging, you will no longer be miserable or unhappy. One essence only exists, which is infinite, spotless, ever pure and completely full. Contemplate upon it and be free from all pain with true calmness of mind.

Become the silent witness

Enter into silence now, from today, in a dark, quiet room. Watch the mind carefully. Be patient. Do not identify with the restless, unbalanced mind. Be a *sakshi* or a silent witness. When there is indifference towards all enjoyments and when the powerful *indriyas* or senses are turned inwards and the *ajnana* or ignorance of the mind is destroyed, only then will all the noble words of the wise men infiltrate the disciple's mind. It is the modifications of the mind, the *vrittis*, that bind one to objects. Be a silent witness to the activities of the mind, and there will no longer be bondage. Be the seer of the mind's dramatic performances and not involved with the mind itself.

When you see a person suffering from colic, you do not feel any pain yourself, but when you get the same colic, you cry out and experience intense agony. Why? Because you identify with the body. If there is no ego identification, you will not feel any pain. This can come only when you become the witness, when there is identification with the Absolute.

Through introspection and contemplation, separate yourself from the thought waves and the fourfold mind:

mind, intellect, subconscious mind and ego, and stand aloof as the witness in your original all blissful nature. Contemplate the words, "I am neither prana nor the senses; I am quite distinct from these. I am the witness of their activities; I am sat-chit-ananda swaroopa." This alone is sufficient for practice. Contemplate the idea that the body is the temple of the radiant and self-effulgent spirit or atma within, which controls all the faculties of the mind and the body. Be aware that you are breathing the breath of the spirit and not a physical breath. You have a body, but you are not the body. You have a mind, but you are not the mind. The body and mind are instruments, like the tools of a carpenter. This body is an instrument or servant of the soul, not its prison. When discrimination dawns, one will see the atman within.

Sit peacefully. Discriminate. Thinking causes identification with the body, 'I-ness' and 'mineness', time and space. Stop this thinking through dispassion and practice and merge yourself in the pure consciousness where there is no thinking. Disassociate from the thoughts and the mind, which is the thinking principle or entity. Identify with the innermost Self and become the silent witness. This is liberation while living. Continue the practice of mental quiet. Only when the subtle desires are annihilated is mental tranquillity possible. Gradually all thoughts will die by themselves. You will become one with the Supreme Self or Para Brahman.

Self-enquiry
Self-enquiry is the effort to keep the mind always concentrated on atman or Brahman, the centre of equilibrium within. Real peace can only be had in one's own Self, where there is neither pleasure nor pain. It is an embodiment of peace. To enjoy the bliss of the Self, the mind will have to be transcended. First conquer the mind through enquiring, 'Who am I?' Until the blissful self-knowledge dawns, sadhana must be practised regularly, and the teachings of the guru and the scriptures followed implicitly. Do not stop thinking of God even for half a second. Become one whose sole refuge

is meditation on *Om* with feeling and meaning. The atman is the only real everlasting abode of perennial peace and deep abiding joy, wherein this fluctuating, restless mind can find permanent rest. Sages like Shankara, Dattatreya, Mansoor, Madalasa, Gargi, Chudalai, Jesus and others reached this destination after strenuous struggle and exertion.

If you can rest in your centre, nothing can affect you and throw you off balance. If you can stay in tune with the Infinite, you will have a poised and balanced mind. A small fishing boat is tossed about hither and thither even by ordinary waves, but a big steamer remains unshaken even though violent waves dash against it with tremendous impetuosity. In the same way, a worldly person with a fickle mind is tossed about even by the small waves of likes and dislikes, whereas a saint with a balanced and serene mind remains in the world without being in the least affected by the stormy waves of troubles and tribulations. He is always resting peacefully in the perpetual calm of the Absolute Self. That state is the yoga of equanimity.

Whenever you are very worried, very depressed or in severe pain, remember that you are the atman, which is the nature of peace and serenity. Withdraw the mind from objects and worldly thoughts and fix it on the atman. Just as you know that flowering mango trees will give mangoes soon, know also that you will attain knowledge of the identity of the Supreme Self or atman when the flower of equanimity blossoms in the mind.

The mind will move inward only when the outgoing tendencies of the mind are arrested, when all its attention is turned on itself alone. An aspirant can do a lot of sadhana when he attains this state. Vairagya and introspection help a lot in the attainment of this mental state. Learn the art of making the mind introspective or turned inward upon itself through pratyahara.

Peace can only be found within, not in external objects. Peace does not come by fretting and fuming. Peace ensues out of calmness and strength. Dive within and introspect.

Search within. See if you are practising the tenets of your own resolve to attain equanimity. If the answer is no, make a firm resolve to do so. Peace of mind is bound to follow as day follows night. Look within. Enter into the great calm or the secret place of the most high.

8

Concentration and Meditation

Through the practices of concentration and meditation, the yogi loses contact with sense objects and comes into contact with the immortal Self within and thus enjoys the supreme peace of Brahman. Aspirants, awaken! Sensual pleasures are transitory or fleeting, but the bliss of Brahman is uninterrupted, undecaying and everlasting. That is the reason why one should attempt to realize the Self within. By concentration and meditation practices the yogi removes the obstacles that stand in the way of obtaining union with the Lord and thus always keeps the mind steady in the Self.

CONCENTRATION

Concentration is the way to get rid of worldly miseries and thus attain a balanced and steady mind. Man is born to practise concentration and through concentration to realize the Self. That is the purpose for which he has taken birth in a human body. However, he forgets this duty due to attachment to family, children, money, power, position, respect, name and fame.

Concentration of mind is one of the most difficult and tedious virtues in the world to achieve. The most outstanding habit of the mind is that it cannot stick to one point without a sustained and devoted effort to spiritual sadhana. If you watch the mind carefully, you will discover that it wanders wildly about like an unchained monkey. Yet, concentration means to unite the rays of the mind at one point, to bring the mind back again and again to one chosen point or idea. So bear in mind that perfect one-pointedness is not achieved in just a day.

Always remember that the effect and the spiritual impressions of a little sadhana will always remain. Nothing is ever lost in sincere sadhana, that is the immutable law of Nature. Practise one-pointedness regularly for one or two years, and be firm in it. You will not be able to detect the slight improvements that come out of a little practice as you do not have a subtle intellect, and have many kinds of impurities from beginningless time. Yet, little by little, the tossing of the mind will quieten down and the state of samadhana will be attained. Mental balance, stability of mind and mental peace will be attained. This is the fruit of constant and protracted sadhana. Do not worry if the mind wanders during the early stages of concentration practice. Be regular. Slowly the mind will automatically turn godward, and once it tastes the bliss of the Self, nothing will be able to shake it.

Concentration purifies and calms the surging emotions and the mind becomes calm, serene and steady. The various rays of the mind are collected and focused on the object of contemplation. There will be no tossing of the mind. The whole energy of the mind is concentrated on one idea and penetrative insight is acquired. The senses become still and do not function.

Steady and systematic practice of raja yoga, beginning with the yamas and niyamas, asana, pranayama and pratyahara will purify and prepare the mind for concentration. Seek out an expert teacher and devote yourself relentlessly to sadhana. The vital point in concentration is to bring the mind to the same point or object again and again, by limiting its movement to a small circle. In the beginning, that is the main aim.

Through dispassion, pratyahara and the practice of concentration, the dissipated rays of the wandering mind are slowly collected. Through steady practice it is rendered one-pointed. After one-pointedness is attained full restraint of the thoughts and emotions needs to be achieved. Then one must continue one's sadhana until all the modifications of the mind subside completely. Eventually the mind will become blank or void. Even then one will have to rise above this void and be ready to contemplate and identify with the silent witness of the mind, known as the Self or Purusha. At this point the aspirant is ready to take up meditation practice, not before.

MEDITATION

If the mind is not kept clean by regular practice of meditation, it becomes unbalanced or impure. Meditation removes the dross of the mind, kills all the pain and suffering and destroys all the causes of sorrow. Learn to exercise supreme control over the nerve currents, muscles, and calm the bubbling emotions, sentiments, instincts and impulses gradually through regular, silent meditation. By gradual and systematic practice, a new orientation can be given to the feelings. The worldly mind can be entirely transmuted into a divine mind, serene and balanced. In this way, meditation allows an aspirant access to the realms of everlasting peace. To purify, to concentrate, to meditate and to realize one's divine essence is the foremost duty of everyone.

During meditation the mind is calm and steady. Perfect harmony, undisturbed happiness and abiding peace will be enjoyed. One will attain the yoga of equanimity, *samatvam*. When meditation becomes deep, perfect awareness and the inner silence of the soul will be experienced. This supreme peace cannot be attained without first having removed the impurities of the mind through japa, service, giving, pranayama, and so on, and then following the path of introspection, contemplation and meditation. Without the help of meditation the veils that cover the soul, the Atman, cannot be removed.

Gradually, reasoning and reflection will give place to awareness. If you can meditate for half an hour, you will be able to engage yourself with peace and spiritual strength in the battle of life for one week through the force of this meditation. Such is the beneficial result of this meditation. Meditation will give you the strength and peace to associate with people of different natures in your daily life without trouble and worry. Sit down with a composed mind, and assert your mastery over the body, mind and senses.

After some months of regular daily meditation practice, the craving or hankering nature of the mind will slowly vanish, and things which used to upset you easily will no longer touch you. You have gained the strength, endurance, resistance and the power to deal with troubles. The whole mind will become quiet. Unkind words will no longer trouble you. Even if you become irritable and show signs of anger, you are now able to compose yourself quickly. These are all signs of gaining mental balance. One who has the power of discrimination is the happiest. He is God himself. His joy is indescribable. He should be adored. Meditation brings about all these beneficial results.

Meditation is keeping up one idea, be it nirguna Brahman, saguna Brahman or an abstract idea. Meditation follows concentration where all the rays of the mind are focused on to a single thought. Ultimately, even this single thought gives place to just awareness and illumination, where all problems dissolve. When one enters into deep meditation, there is no consciousness of one's body or surroundings. No sounds will be heard. The consciousness of egoism also will gradually vanish. If one frees oneself from the clutches of the mind, samatvam will come by itself. There is no doubt about this. By meditation on God, pure thoughts emanate from the mind, because God is purity. If one has control over the thoughts, then mental torments, cares, worries and anxieties will disappear. All the processes of worldly life, all the miseries of births and deaths will then come to an end. You will attain equanimity of mind. Inexplicable serenity and indescribable happiness will be experienced. My child! Meditate. Come into the deep, deep quiet. Come into the profound, infinite silence or peace.

9

Karma Yoga

Serve

Through love, unselfish service and selfless giving, all the conflicting aspects of the personality can be united and equanimity attained. Serving others balances the mind and emotions. Therefore, as the aspirant goes about his daily life, he should hold the attitude that his duty is to serve others. By means of selfless and humble service to the poor and the afflicted, the heart can be purified and made a fit abode for God to dwell in. Losing the sense of 'I'-ness and 'mine'-ness will help the aspirant to control his own mind, even his entire personality.

Fix the mind on the Lord and give the hands to worldly activities. Always repeat the name of the Lord while at work. Through gradual practice one will be able to keep a portion of the mind engaged in japa and meditation on the Lord, while another portion will be on one's work, which is actually worship of Him. This is karma yoga and bhakti yoga combined. There is no need to retire from worldly life. Samatvam can be realized even while remaining in the world if this method is adopted. This is the master key to open the doors of the realms of supreme peace. This is the secret of karma yoga, and the secret of success in samatvam yoga.

Work elevates the aspirant who serves with the spirit of selflessness. There is a peculiar joy and bliss in this practice.

While working, especially with others, watch every action and reaction within yourself. In the beginning, all your actions may be selfish. Scrutinize your motives, purify them and struggle hard. When anything pricks your conscience, abandon it, and do not be tempted by the power of self-gratification and self-aggrandizement.

While working, endeavour to overcome anger by love, falsehood by truth, greed by generosity and pride by humility. Every day is a fresh beginning. Forget past mistakes and failures. After some years of hard, incessant struggle, your actions will become purely unselfish. Enter a new life of victory over the mind. March on and on. Be up and doing! Exert. Purify.

Worldly-minded people cannot understand the spirit of selfless service. The mind is so framed that it cannot work without expecting fruits or anticipating rewards for actions. Passionate beings cannot dream of doing any work without expecting some gain for themselves and their family. They are always tense and worried that events will not work out in their favour. This is the inborn nature of a worldly-minded person.

How can a person do karma yoga if he is extremely selfish, if he has no self-restraint? If you want everything for yourself, if you are luxurious and have not reduced your wants, how can you spare something for others? The mind will never find balance and peace. However, when the thought of doing good to others becomes part and parcel of one's very being, then one will take immense delight in serving others without any expectation of rewards. An underlying sense of contentment and quietness will be felt within.

Surely one can take the initiative to serve and do good to others! Knowledge can be imparted to the illiterate and the ignorant, monetary help extended to the poor and the needy, orphans educated and contributions made to the institutions that care for them. Indeed, one can always provide something useful and beneficial to others. Why should there be any hesitation in regard to being really helpful to others? Free the mind of all restrictions. By serving others, the mind will become serene and the heart will be happy.

Love

Serve everyone with intense love, without the idea of doership. By working for others without expecting appreciation, one learns to be kind and compassionate. Develop all-embracing love. Feel for others as you feel for yourself. Feeling oneness with others is *atmabhava*. Unite with all and feel the calmness within. Separation is death, imbalance, conflict and dissatisfaction. Unity is eternal serenity, composure and happiness. This sadhana will give unimaginable peace of mind. Expand your heart and think that this whole world is your own Self.

An aspirant should also learn thought transference, the method of sending out a continuous stream of healing, loving and helpful thoughts to others and the whole world at large. This is silent, selfless service to humanity. You should know how to remove distraction and collect all your thoughts and send them out as a battalion of helpful forces to do good to those who are suffering. Just as the Ganga brings joy and coolness to those who live on its banks, so also one's strong thoughts of love and peace must flow out as a healing stream to bring solace and peace to those whose minds are filled with cares and worries.

Love expects no reward. Love knows no fear. Divine love gives; it does not demand. Love thinks no evil, imputes no motive. To love is to share and serve. Worshipping God in others will bring the great quality of mental peace, which will allow you to remain equipoised. Thus you will be able to achieve the goal for which God has given this human body. Selfless work elevates and brings freedom to the mind and emotions. Selfish work unbalances the mind and retards spiritual progress. Working without any kind of motive leads to purity and inner strength. Become a *nishkama karma* yogi, one who dedicates all actions to God. What an expanded heart you will have!

61

When discrimination dawns, when the mind is filled with more purity, the spirit of selflessness begins to grow slowly. The mind has to be tamed very cautiously to work in a disinterested manner. While engaged in selfless service, an insidious feeling of self-approbation may creep in unnoticed. This may later manifest in the form of an indulgent attitude and a lofty contempt for those who are not following a similar life. Constant humility kept alive by ceaselessly exercising it in serving others is the sure armour against this foe. Discipline the mind with patience and perseverance.

If you find it difficult to work without any motive, have one strong pure motive when you work – to worship God. This will destroy all the other lower selfish motives, which will eventually die by themselves. The inner peace and joy gained from selfless activities is boundless. If the motive is pure, purity of mind will be obtained. If the motive is impure, if you expect fruit for your actions, you will have to return to this world to reap those fruits. You will be entrapped in the neverending wheel of births and deaths.

Give

Give in plenty, in humility and with joy. In the very process of giving you will enrich yourself too. Peace of mind comes to one who gives joy and happiness to others. Give of yourself for the wellbeing of the world. Only through selfless activities, unattached work and loving service can one acquire the precious gems of purity, patience and humility which lead to equanimity. Giving and not identifying with actions purifies the mind and heart and prepares one to receive divine grace and spiritual peace.

For a beginner, selfless service is easier than self-enquiry, jnana yoga. It purifies the heart and prepares the mind for the attainment of *Atma jnana*, knowledge of the Self. By gradual practice and purification of the mind, you can become an expert in karma yoga. True nishkama yogis are able to remain unshaken by grief and loss, anger and malice, lust and greed, hatred and jealousy. They are always calm and serene though engaged in ceaseless action. Thus they always maintain a balanced mind. In this manner all their actions are done perfectly and selflessly. The karma yogi should take up jnana yoga as soon as his heart and mind are purified. This is the goal of selfless service. All his actions will then culminate in *jnana*, or spiritual wisdom. Karma, bhakti and raja yogas are a means to the end, Atma jnana. Just as rivers join the sea, so also karma, bhakti and raja yogas join the ocean of jnana yoga.

Perform action for purification
Plunge into selfless service. Actions done unselfishly, purely in service of the Lord, do not bind the devotee and purify the heart. Otherwise your actions will bind you to *samsara*, the wheel of births and deaths, however good or glorious they may be. Have equal vision and a balanced mind in success and failure, in heat and cold, in honour and dishonour, in pleasure and pain, in happiness and sorrow. If you give up selfishness, meanness, attachment and egoism, you will be free from the bonds of karma. Supreme peace, eternal bliss and immortality will be attained. This is the yoga of equanimity, *samatvam*.

Be ever active and at the same time feel inwardly that you are the non-doer and non-enjoyer. Take a deep interest in everything and yet be perfectly unattached. Lord Krishna asks us to act, but to act only with devotion to Him and without desire for the fruits of the actions. "See Me in everything. Surrender yourself to Me. Do all actions for My sake. Cut off attachments. Have perfect, unswerving devotion to Me. Sing My glories." Live in the spirit of these teachings.

Once you have tasted the bliss of selfless service, you can never leave it. You will begin to feel that this whole world is a manifestation of God. The spirit of self-sacrifice will grow. Immense faith, inner strength and purity of heart will be gained. The heart will be filled with sympathy, mercy and pure love. Selfishness, greed, egoism, feelings of superiority, vanity, pride, and hatred contract the heart and stand in the way of developing peace of mind. Melt and destroy the barriers that separate one human being from another.

Feel that the whole world is your body, your own home. Even after years of intense sadhana, equal vision and equipoise cannot be attained unless jealousy, backbiting and all forms of selfishness are removed from the ego. It is nonsense to say, "I am meditating for six hours daily." First the mind must be purified through selfless service for an extended period.

Do not wrestle or struggle with the mind. Constant selfless service with atmabhava is highly efficacious in balancing the mind. Serve, love, and give. By excelling in selfless service, supreme tranquillity of mind is experienced. Alongside selfless service, be regular in concentration and meditation. May peace, joy, bliss and immortality abide in you for ever and ever! Om Shanti, Shanti, Shanti!

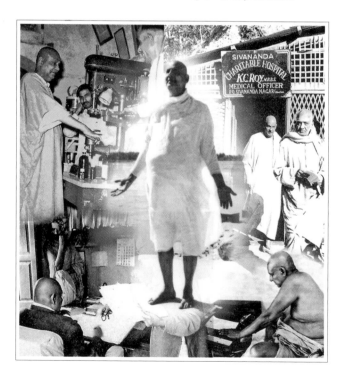

Samatvam

From the teachings of Swami Satyananda Saraswati

10

A Philosophy of Samatvam

The spiritual aspirant has to become an expert at living between the positive and negative events of life. Sometimes there is success and sometimes failure. Both knock you about this way and that. Happiness throws you over to unhappiness and unhappiness throws you back to happiness, and you are kicked about like a football from one to the other. In order to obtain balance of mind, you do not have to change your life – you just have to develop a new kind of philosophy.

Philosophical detachment
What is that philosophy? If we call it detachment, that does not cover the entire philosophy of yoga because externally you will remain in the thick and thin of life, and not abandon even one item. Your work, relationships, fruits of action, consequences, reversals and defeats all have to be experienced. You cannot escape or reject any experiences. If you try to ignore them in your waking hours, they will live with you in sleep and in dreams. They will follow you throughout your life because you have to work them all out.

Every experience is valuable. Even if you are suffering because of your husband, wife, children or friends, or because of certain complexes like inferiority, superiority and narcissism, or you have guilt or sin or a perverse sexual nature, you have to manage it. It does not matter if you are arrogant and obstinate, or very good and charitable, or if you exploit or are exploited by your friends, you have to learn from that experience. You do not have to fight with your attachments, or to force detachment, but you must be able to find a way through.

Mental balance is a sadhana

Rather than philosophical detachment, it is more appropriate to call this philosophy mental balance. Detachment takes time to develop; it is not so easy that you can start doing it from today. It is not just saying, "No, I am not related to you; I am not attached to you." You are related to everybody: father, mother, sisters, brothers and cousins, and from time to time things happen between people which damage the mind and completely destroy its mental structure. As a result, one's perspective on life can be thrown completely off balance, and then everything goes out of order. However, one cannot proceed on the spiritual path with a damaged mind. So it is more apt to name this philosophy mental balance for the reason that every aspirant must be very careful to hold the mind steady under all conditions.

Always aim to attain and maintain mental balance. Things keep coming and they will touch you, yet you must still keep moving. Somehow you must be able to remain above all the clamour. Do not allow anything to overwhelm you. Do not worry! It may be impossible to be one hundred percent true to your convictions at all times, but still you should try because nothing should injure your mind. Mental balance is a sadhana; it is a means of taking care of the mind. Our relationships have always been tense and painful, creating fears, sorrows, tensions, stress and many other experiences, but that should change. Experiences come and go and one should learn to observe them and to become the witness.

Understanding the witness

Mental equilibrium is maintained by remaining a witness. One definition of yoga is: an art by which we become a spectator of all the experiences of awareness. It is almost a process of disunion, for when we begin to expand our awareness and become the witness, we are separating ourselves from our external consciousness. When consciousness functions through the senses, it is called sense consciousness; when it functions through the mind, it is called mind consciousness and so on, but when consciousness functions without any obscuring filter, then it is known as cosmic awareness, divine awareness, transcendental awareness.

Knowledge, incorrect knowledge and absence of knowledge are the individual forms of consciousness which we experience every day. They are patterns of consciousness which function through mediums. If you listen to my lecture, your awareness is functioning through the auditory medium. If I am looking at you and you are looking at me, our consciousness is functioning through the ocular medium. If you are thinking about my lecture, your consciousness is functioning through the intellectual medium. In these ways the pure, formless and nameless awareness has a form and a name.

Who experiences pain and pleasure? Who understands things and who makes mistakes? It is the individual, pure awareness, but through various mediums or filters. This pure consciousness is like formless light in front of which a film is running of perception, audition, feeling, knowing, moving, understanding and incorrect understanding. We see everything that is taking place in front of us, for this world is a play of perceptions, an experience of perceptions, an expression of consciousness through mediums or filters. When these filters are removed, there is no life, no perception. There is only one experience, which never ceases to exist. It exists without interruption in all places and in all circumstances, at all times, whether mediums or filters are there or not.

The fact is that my consciousness, your consciousness, consciousness itself can exist, will exist and has been existing eternally. Yogis knew the certainty of the continuation of consciousness. They discovered that in every being there is something which can exist without any medium and they started trying to work out ways to develop that state at will, voluntarily. In yoga this is what is meant by being the witness. We can define yoga, therefore, as a process by which we can make our consciousness free from any medium of knowledge or identification.

Try to understand that everything you come across in life, every person and event, is actually neutral in nature. It is neither the source of pain nor the source of joy, but due to a defective philosophy you have suffered and attributed your suffering to these events, objects and persons. In your new philosophy, an absolute distinction has to be made whereby no object, event, person or experience can become a source of positive or negative response, where nothing can disturb your equipoise. This is the philosophy of samatvam yoga.

Live like a lotus

When this new philosophy comes into your life, externally everything remains the same, but the relationships with each and everything you are related to change. This change is for a great spiritual purpose – to attain peace and equanimity of mind. This peace leads to the highest bliss and liberation from the bondage of worldly existence.

One has to live like a lotus in water. A lotus is born in water, lives in water and survives by water but remains absolutely dry. We are all born into the world and survive by the world because without the world there is nothing. There is no noise in the world; there is no peace in the Himalayas! Both are within you. You can attain the highest yoga, you can have the darshan of God, if you can make your mind still and peaceful. While it is true that one can have darshan of God even at home, it is also a fact that one can find peace in the world as well.

Try to understand the depth, universality and eternity of your nature through life itself. Perfect happiness and supreme peace are experienced only after one has introspected and analyzed oneself and then taken to the path of sadhana and thus determined to lead a virtuous and divine life. The process leading to the state of samatvam is an art, a method of wrestling with one's own mind. It is a process of becoming the witness, and a process through which one frees the mind from its limitations. In the final state of this process one gains light, peace, tranquillity, understanding, wisdom, joy and bliss.

The art of equanimity is a virtue in itself. It must be complete. It is essential for the beginner to have faith in higher possibilities, to keep on removing unnecessary thoughts, to correct the mind, and to become the detached witness. This material world should be accepted without attachment or aversion. Always remind yourself: that which is favourable for attaining supreme consciousness should be accepted and that which is unfavourable should be rejected. That is called *samata*, equanimity.

11

How to Attain Equanimity

To attain equanimity of mind, sages and thinkers down through the ages have been teaching us to live in this world like the tongue lives amongst a set of thirty-two teeth. How perilous is its condition. At any moment the tongue can be bitten to pieces, but despite this, it manages to remain unharmed. Similarly, human beings should be as dexterous as the tongue and learn to live in the midst of life's struggles without being affected, to face all the ups and downs, hopes and despairs, without being tainted. Not allowing the mind to be affected negatively by the contradictions of life is the yoga of equanimity.

Contradiction is the law of life, progress and mobility. There is contradiction everywhere in creation; there is no uniform philosophy in life. If there were no contradictions or adverse situations, there would be no progress or evolution. The very fact of existence itself is a contradiction. Therefore, rather than worrying about the various contradictions in our life, whether emotional, mental or intellectual, we need to find a way of accepting contradictions and conflicts, and still remain harmonious and balanced.

Have a goal and a philosophy of life

If people know and somehow experience that life has a spiritual purpose, and have a goal and a philosophy of divine life to live by so as to attain that purpose, then all will be well. One must be involved in life, but at the same time one must develop a deeper, higher, more perpetual, enduring and abiding awareness.

In order to live according to a higher philosophy, one needs a yogic base. Take up a yogic philosophy of *vairagya*, non-attachment or dispassion, *dhyana*, meditation, and *anasakti*, the process of detachment. These concepts symbolize a dynamic approach to life and the very purpose of existence. A householder often has no higher goal or philosophy, he is just living. However, the true goal and final destiny of mankind cannot be property, material wealth, provident funds, begetting children and educating them. Although human beings experience unlimited desires, ambitions and passions, which should not be denied, it is the soul or *atman* which has to be realized.

We cannot regard an individual as just a citizen, a patriot, a father, a mother, an employee, or a member of society. Rather we should consider the spirit as being the substratum of all the other roles we play in life. As far as total cosmic existence is concerned a spiritual aspirant has only one destination – self-realization. When you realize that this is the purpose of your human incarnation, you will become a sincere seeker of eternal peace and you will work to become liberated from the endless cycle of karma.

Have patience

To achieve the state of equanimity, try to integrate and harmonize both the internal and external elements of life. To do this, there is actually nothing to give up, nothing to reject. As you evolve, many habits, addictions and experiences are left behind. As you grow older, your hair goes grey and your teeth fall out; it is a natural process. In the same way, what we call the sensualities of life, the infirmities of willpower, the habits and weaknesses will all fall away one by one by themselves, without you having to do anything.

We are all subject to the laws of universal or cosmic nature, and according to those laws we have a certain type

of personality, a certain way of thinking, a certain kind of
conviction, and certain types of strengths and weaknesses
from time to time. But we should not worry about it or try
to get out of it. We should wait. We must have patience. If
we have patience, we will find that in the course of time,
like a snake, those scales will be thrown off automatically or
will eventually drop away because habits and addictions are
transitory. All the thoughts that go through the mind are
impermanent; they keep moving like a flowing river.

Respect yourself

Every spiritual aspirant must respect his own personality
completely. You should never suffer from guilt complexes,
sin and negativity. You are an integral part of the cosmic
drama and, therefore, you are playing your part. Once you
are convinced about your stage in life and have respect for
yourself, for your physical body, for your wife, husband
and children, state of mind, moral philosophy, ethics and
religion, you will make rapid spiritual progress. However,
if you suffer from inferiority complexes, you will constantly
be thinking, "I am not a good person, I am evil minded, I
am weak, I am sensual, I am not fit for spiritual life." These
kinds of thoughts do not belong to a spiritual aspirant who
aspires to yoga. This attitude does nothing to harmonize or
balance the mind and body. Whether you are sensual, anti-
sensual or hypo-sensual does not matter, accept it! Then
whatever form of yoga you do will produce astounding
results and give you experiences very fast.

Be regular in sadhana

First, have respect for your lifestyle and your personality, and
second, be regular in your sadhana, at any cost! Every day
without fail, with absolute regularity, devote a minimum of ten
minutes to your yoga practice so as to connect with your inner
nature, with that place of stillness, silence and peace within.
There is no need to think, "Oh, my mind is not steady, my
mind is not tranquil, my mind is not one-pointed." This is the

most important part of sadhana, whether you are well or ill, whether or not you have faith, whether or not you understand, whether or not you get results.

It is very difficult to maintain regularity in spiritual practice for at least a few years. It is not difficult to take up yoga and to start practising sadhana, but to continue is difficult. To establish regularity takes time, not just six months. It can easily take two or three years, after which you can say, "Yes, regularity has been established. Now I can go ahead with three hours of sadhana." In that lies the secret of one's success.

For ten minutes, sit calmly and quietly, with the body absolutely still, with the eyes closed, and gaze inward, either at the nosetip, the mid-eyebrow centre, the heart centre or the navel centre. Fix your inner gaze at one of these points. You can practise your mantra, meditation on a form or symbol, concentration on the breath or on the light at the mid-eyebrow centre, on your symbol in the heart or in the navel centre, at whatever point you have chosen for this practice. If you have time, practise more. Whatever you practise, however, remember that regularity is of the greatest importance. It is not the quantum of practice, but regularity which will ultimately give inner peace and equanimity of mind.

Continually analyze yourself to see how the knocks of life are affecting your inner state of mind, the divine quality within you. An aspirant's life must be of such nobility and so fulfilling that the onslaughts, tremors and shocks from family, friends and enemies just do not affect him. If these things draw your awareness, you must be aware of them, but at the same time remain unshaken. You will find that your mind spontaneously attains tranquillity. Whether your philosophy is based on religion, on raja yoga or on bhakti, it must emerge from the depths of your heart, so that one day when you sit for meditation, your consciousness shoots up like a rocket and goes to the highest point of samadhi.

12

Samatvam and Disidentification

To attain samatvam, the mind must be made stronger and less vulnerable to external impressions and crises. The mind must be strengthened so that adverse outside events no longer disturb its functioning. Most people are like fragile glass balls; they crack, shatter or go to pieces every time they are bounced by a difficult life situation. But in life one must become like a rubber ball.

If you throw a rubber ball on the ground, it will rebound without any detrimental change to its inner composition. You must be like this rubber ball, resilient, yet strong, flexible in all situations, and yet without allowing the upheavals of life to touch the inner core of your being. This is easier said than done, but the method of watching situations as though they are something apart from you is a great aid to gaining inner stability.

Try to disidentify as much as possible with your body, emotions and mind. Detachment is an excellent method of bringing this about. Although one acts out and reacts to external roles, activities and feelings of love, hate and anger, they should be seen as something outside oneself. These external activities should not be allowed to affect you in a deeper sense. You must be aware of them as though you are a witness.

Be aware of everything that happens. Act like a witness, without identifying yourself with anything. Over-identification with the body, emotions and mind will lead to painful and undesirable physical, emotional and mental experiences. Try to watch all the activities from the centre of consciousness. In this way sorrowful events and any other events will not leave a mark on your inner being. They will occur as though they are something different and apart from you. The ripples and waves will disturb the surface of the lake, but leave the depths still, calm and undisturbed. One must aim to be aware, as an observer under all circumstances, including even the most tumultuous, agitated or disturbing conditions. It can be done quite easily during the practice of asanas, pranayama, and so on, but to maintain this attitude during everyday activities requires effort and practice.

Over-identification

Much unhappiness is the result of over-identification with the body, emotions and mind. The same applies to over-identification with one's work, or role in life. A process of disidentification is necessary as a method of obtaining tranquillity. It is strange that if people are asked what they are, they will usually reply, "I am an engineer", or "I am a doctor", or "I am a secretary", or perhaps, "I am a housewife." They will answer according to what they identify with in life, what their role, work or preoccupation is.

This over-identification applies in almost everyone's life. Consider a mother. She identifies with her role; she sees herself only as a mother, nothing else. Yet eventually her children will probably leave home, just as young birds will leave the nest. If she has totally identified with the role of a mother, then she will suffer much unhappiness. If one over-identifies with all the roles that one assumes, then they will definitely cause anguish and emotional upset when the role finishes or changes.

It is possible to watch the activities of the body, emotions and mind as a spectator. If you have never experienced this, then you have missed something very revealing. The body, emotions and mind are merely instruments of something deeper, and they are certainly not the real 'I'. The 'I' that witnesses is the 'I' to identify with. If you can do this, then your body and mind will function more efficiently, unhampered by prejudices, fears, and so on. You will attain wonderful physical and mental health.

If you want to gain more relaxation and flow with the current of life, rather than being in a continual state of strife with the impressions of the environment throwing you upside down, then you must realize that your roles in life are only actions, nothing more. They are not that part of you which is immortal or permanent. Continue to perform all actions, but look at them from a new perspective. Consider yourself as an actor performing the roles. Your deeper self or nature will be the audience, while the body and mind will carry out the roles.

Next, you must try to disidentify with your body, emotions and personal mind while remaining aware of them. This is not easy and at first it will only be intellectual, but with practice you will find that you identify with them less and less. This is not surprising for the witness is consciousness. You are not creating anything; you are merely allowing that which is already there to reassert itself in your being.

Inner and outer harmony
There are a large number of techniques for cleaning out the mind and inducing tranquillity. In psychiatry there are methods such as initiated symbol projection, dream interpretation, and picture association. The basic problem of lack of meaning in life will dissolve and disappear in the course of making progress in yoga. Another factor is to follow your own aspiration in life. As much as possible express your talents through work or play, as this also helps to eliminate mental strife, for one becomes caught in a flow of concentrated activity. External expression is a necessary part of exhausting mental problems. Also practise karma yoga, selfless action, so that you do not become too preoccupied with yourself.

Both in the past and the present, human beings have devoted most of their attention to mastering outer events, caring little for inner events. There has to be a progressive movement towards harmony, both in the internal and external worlds. Internal problems must be progressively erased from the subconscious mind. The experiences of disidentification with the mind, body and emotions by becoming the witness, the 'I', will hasten this process until the accumulated 'dust' of past conditioning and impediments is wiped from the mind. Then you will know what Christ meant when he talked about 'the peace that passes all understanding'.

13

Striving For Steadiness
of Mind

The *Bhagavad Gita* has eighteen chapters. The name of the last chapter is 'Moksha Sannyasa Yoga', renunciation of all karmas, supreme peace and liberation. The title of the first chapter is 'The Yoga of Despondency'. Can you believe that despondency, dejection and frustration can also be yoga, that they can be a means for the development of consciousness? It is accepted that karma yoga, bhakti yoga, raja yoga, jnana yoga, hatha yoga, laya yoga, mantra yoga, kriya yoga and other yogas purify the consciousness. But how can imbalances of mind, body, intellect and psyche, how can disappointment and a completely broken heart be the means for the evolution of inner consciousness? That is the primary hypothesis of the *Bhagavad Gita*, one of the most important spiritual texts given to humankind.

The *Bhagavad Gita* is, in fact, a thesis on *samatvam*, on the yoga of equanimity. In the opening chapter, when Arjuna saw the two armies of his relatives flanked on the battlefield, he became disillusioned with life and refused to fight. Then Lord Krishna gave him instructions as to how he should act, and these instructions contain the essence of samatvam yoga.

Most people believe that yoga begins with discipline and self-control, with yama and niyama, asana and pranayama, but this is not so. Yoga begins at that moment when one is facing calamities, when one is in total darkness and yet trying to manage oneself. The *Bhagavad Gita* contends that yoga begins when you are facing great disappointments, when you are totally disillusioned with life, when you are at breaking point, when you are depressed and facing nervous breakdown, when your mind is full of conflict and you are being pulled equally from both sides, when tears flow from your eyes, when your heart is full of agony and anguish, when you do not know exactly what to do, when you become angry and want to run away or commit suicide, when you know the truth but cannot accept it.

Find a positive solution
What do you do at such a time? Many people surrender completely to such difficult situations, but most try to maintain their balance and find a positive solution. This attempt to overcome the situation is the beginning of yoga, defined by Lord Krishna as samatvam, the yoga of equanimity.

Once we take birth in this physical body, we are subject to the laws of nature. We cannot get away from it despite our struggles to do so. *Maya* or illusion, and *avidya* or ignorance, always follow man like a shadow throughout his life, and sometimes overpower him. Even people of great wisdom, who have led lives of austerity and discipline, who have experienced divinity, often become victims of avidya and lose their equanimity. Remember that the body and its karma, the mind and its karma, mundane existence and its karma surround us everywhere and always.

When you are living a mundane life and performing your karmas, you must analyze and understand the fleeting qualities of that life and then try to understand what gifts striving in mundane life has given you. It has given the sense of disillusionment, out of which comes the gift of realization or a better understanding of the worldly and spiritual paths. The human birth which has been ordained to us is not a punishment, but a chance, an opportunity given to evolve and attain enlightenment.

Trying to assert your mind during times of trouble is the first chapter of yoga in your life. The yoga of equanimity does not begin with a religious, philosophical or puritanical discipline or with self-control nor with giving up of wine, meat and smoking. The very first step is when you become aware of the depression and disturbance in your life and try your level best to find a balance. Everyone faces this balancing act amidst the mundane activities of life. It is striving for steadiness of mind, a sense that there must be something more to life. It is the primary and preliminary step into the yoga of equanimity.

Those who consider the performance of mundane actions and spiritual life to be two separate compartments do not see the truth behind existence. There can only be one truth, not two. Improve and heighten the quality of your awareness so you can realize that you are not the body but something more than that. Then you must transcend pain and sorrow, fights and quarrels. If you practise the different yogas to evolve your consciousness, then you can eventually transcend everything, even yourself. This striving is the process of samatvam.

The whole of life is a process of samatvam yoga. You cannot divide life into two different compartments. You cannot say, "This is yoga and that is not yoga." Yoga is not only the practice of asana, pranayama and meditation. Whatever you do, whatever you eat, whatever you give and take and whatever suffering and happiness you undergo, all that is samatvam yoga. From dawn to dusk, whatever way you choose to live is the yoga by which you endeavour to attain contentment and peace of mind, even when your body is ailing, or when your lover has deserted you, or when the situation is very hard.

Balancing material and spiritual life

In the Vedas, the rishis and munis indicated four kinds of striving which would allow human beings to express every facet of their personality and enjoy the different stages of life, and to finally achieve the purpose for which they were born. *Dharma* means virtuous qualities, performing good actions and good deeds. *Artha* means material need and its attainment. *Kama* means desires and their fulfilment. *Moksha* means liberation from everything, when the mind transcends itself and attains the state of supreme peace.

For a householder, artha and kama are the prominent extrovert behaviours, and dharma and moksha are the internal, inherent qualities or spiritual inspirations. For a karma sannyasin or a sannyasin, dharma and moksha are the prominent inspirations, and artha and kama are the means to achieve them. In this way a synthesis has to be achieved; it is a natural process of spiritual evolution from birth to death.

Brahmacharya ashrama, student life, leads to *grihastha ashrama,* householder life. Grihastha ashrama leads to *vanaprastha ashrama,* retirement, and vanaprastha ashrama leads to *sannyasa ashrama,* liberation from the cycle of karma, birth and death. If you can perceive the purpose behind these four *ashramas* or stages of life, you will understand that you do not have to leave home and do this or that to live a spiritual life. These ashramas are the automatic developments of the philosophy and thought within your mind.

For the first fifteen to twenty-five years of life you strive to acquire knowledge; you prepare yourself by suppressing your petty desires for sensual fulfilment so that you may become a scholar or attain a degree. Then you enter into grihastha ashrama where you face the onslaughts of passions and desires, frustrations and attachments, hatred and love, and adjust yourself every now and then. Sometimes you have accidents, of course, but you are trying your level best to overcome this state of conflict and confrontation and maintain your sense of equilibrium.

In the *Yoga Vasishtha*, Sage Vasishtha explains to Rama the path of transcending the mind. He explains time, space, object, idea, imagination, emotion, and their relationship to spiritual progress and also to bondage. He says, "Rama, you will have to work to become king and rule your subjects. You will have to perform your karma by administrating, maintaining proper law and order and many other duties. There is no harm in that, but remember that everything is an idea, identification with the impermanent reality. Jnana is an idea and karma is an idea; renunciation is an idea and so are desires and passions. Even spiritual experience is an idea. After all, the whole world is maya. Even though you will rule a kingdom, it should not stand in the way of your spiritual life."

Spiritual aspirants must understand what Sage Vasishtha told Rama. When you identify with karma, you suffer and lose your mental and emotional balance. So karma itself is not the cause of suffering. True renunciation is being able to witness all that comes and goes in life. That is the key principle which an aspirant must live by to attain the yoga of equanimity.

Live life fully

Participate in all events externally, but internally maintain an attitude of non-doership. Remember, there is not one, but many levels of experience. In each level you have what appear to be real experiences, but when you transcend that level, then those experiences have no validity. Seemingly valid and real experiences which balance or unbalance the mind are those with which the mind identifies, nothing more.

When you lose the stance of the witness, you become involved with karma, which is the cause of suffering. You identify and thereby suffer because you unbalance your mind, body and intellect and create more karma, more lifetimes of bondage to worldly existence. This identification with karma is a kind of neurosis inherent in the mind. To transcend it, one must take care of one's innate identifications, rather than reacting obsessively for or against one's karma. The *Bhagavad Gita*, *Yoga Vasishtha* and the vedic texts all tell us that mental balance is an essential item of sadhana. It is a quality of understanding the futility and perishability of every type of event. Equilibrium is that quality when you have become a witness of all events.

Mundane life and spiritual life are not two separate compartments. It is you who is experiencing material life and it is you who wants to experience spiritual life. From mundane life to spiritual or yogic life there is a bridge and it is not a no man's land. That bridge is a process which relates to the evolution of your consciousness. It is a process of purification of the mind, intellect, ego and emotions. That bridge is the practice of yoga: karma yoga, raja yoga, bhakti, jnana yoga and so on, whichever yoga suits your temperament.

Every situation that comes into your life is meant to change you and accelerate your evolution. So do not accuse destiny. Do not say that God has cursed you. Pain purifies you. If you suffer from physical disease, you will learn to live in a healthier way. If you misbehave and get into trouble, you will learn how to behave better. Internally you will have to do a lot of overhauling. All the changes are taking place within you, not outside. Of course, it does not happen overnight; it is a gradual process over thousands of lifetimes. Nevertheless, try to understand that every element in life is a part of yoga, part of a process of purification to exhaust the dross, density and thickness of karma, and eventually achieve a state of absolute equilibrium.

14

Balance of Mind and Karma Yoga

If one is able to balance the mind in pleasure and pain, in gain and loss, in praise and criticism, one will never experience grief and agony. However, to attain this balance, the nature of karma and its effect on the mind and external behaviour needs to be understood. With this appreciation one will then need to redefine one's relationship with the karma one is involved in.

Karma means action. Every karma is an outcome of a previous karma and, at the same time, every karma gives birth to a new seed, which is again responsible for the next karma. It is this chain of karma which is invariably linked to every moment of life, and which binds man to an endless cycle of births and deaths. Whenever karma is performed through the mind or the body, a seed is produced in the deeper recesses of the mind and becomes a part of the personality. That seed is an impression, known in yoga as *samskara*, and it remains in a dormant, potential state in the mind, known as the seed state. It is that seed karma which again comes up and influences one's psychological apparatus, behaviour, temperament, inclinations and ambitions. It is responsible for happiness and unhappiness, for successes and failures, for deep-rooted neuroses and complexes, and, of course, for enjoyments. That seed karma influences one's whole life.

It is also very important for aspirants to understand that every karma in life, every relationship, every thought and every enterprise bears mixed results. Both desired and undesired results will happen as a result of your actions. You cannot eliminate this process and you cannot eliminate the possibility of negative and mixed results, because they have to happen. If you consider your own life, you will agree that these mixed results can happen both at the same time, simultaneously, or sometimes one after the other.

Attachment to karma creates bondage

Attachment to karma creates impressions, governs the mind and rules over the willpower. As a result the mind and emotions become so completely shattered and remain in such a state of turmoil that one is unable to adjust or adapt to prevailing circumstances. If karma is performed with this ordinary outlook, then it causes more and more bondage. This chain of karma is an eternal cycle, one that replays itself again and again in the lives of worldly-minded people, until they redefine their relationship with karma.

The way out of this eternal cycle of karma is through the practice of *karma yoga*, the yoga of detached karma, or the yoga of unselfish action. If you do not redefine your relationship with karma, it will keep you in absolute bondage and shackles. You can never become free of your karma unless you perform it with the disinterested attitude of a karma yogi. Even if you run a business successfully for thirty years, you will still feel insecure. This insecurity relates not only to your business affairs, it also concerns your love for your wife and children, or any service you are attached to.

In this manner a kind of error is created in the mind, because the moment you become aware of the karma you also become aware of the results. Certainly, no one will want negative results, or his affairs to fail. Nobody with a family will say, "Oh, let everything deteriorate!' By nature man wants everything to happen in a positive way. If the fruits are good, it is easy to accept. However, one must know how to manage the mind and keep it balanced if the results of the karma are negative.

Spiritual philosophy of karma yoga

If the same karma is done without obsessions, if it is performed with a clear conscience and a detached attitude, and with a calm and quiet mind, it becomes karma yoga. For example, if you plant some seedlings and they freeze during the night, your plans to grow a garden fail. You become frustrated and it breaks your heart. As a result your whole psychological personality is affected and your behaviour and relationship with your family and society and with yourself are influenced. A person's will may be strong or weak, depending upon his past karma.

If the same tragedy is faced by a person of steady mind and understanding, he will react differently. He will not suffer frustration or heartbreak because he knows that he can make another attempt and be successful. So one needs to be able to see how one's reactions can completely put a veil over the eyes of wisdom and lead to wrong judgements and perspectives. One must be able to keep the mind free or detached from the results of karma so that one does not become tainted. If one's mind is always calm and peaceful, one will be able to find a positive way out of any crisis. This sense of internal and spiritual detachment is the main principle in the philosophy and practice of karma yoga, and if practised correctly, many psychological problems can be overcome.

It seems to us that the karma is moving the body, but if you make a deeper analysis, you will realize that every karma is an expression of consciousness, of the mind. If you desire to go to London or to run a business or to hate or love someone, and you do that, you will either succeed or fail. Whatever happens as a result of your undertaking is a kind of manifestation. Karma is the gross manifestation of the subtle forces that are working within human beings.

If you have the vision of a yogi, you will see thousands and thousands of cobwebs inside the deeper realms of your personality, in your behaviour, thinking and attitude to work. Your ego is terrible! You are unaware that your relationships with karma are not properly defined. You are unable to adjust to anyone and it is not possible for anyone to adjust to you. You always find fault with people. You are very attached to karma, and on the higher spiritual plane you are accumulating karma, which is in turn influencing your personality. This type of imbalance in perception happens only because you do not understand the spiritual philosophy of karma yoga.

Here is a clue to the secrets of karma yoga and equanimity of mind. One has to perform karma, but try to become free from it at the same time. How is that possible when you have so much work to do, when you have to meet people of many different temperaments? You think that to be successful you should exert your ego and individuality, but that is not the way. Not only will your spiritual progress be blocked, you will also remain unhappy and create more karma.

You may say that karma begets sins and more karma and, therefore, you do not want to work. However, nobody can renounce karma, even if one retires to the Himalayas for years. Karma must be done and is done by every one of us, continuously throughout our lives. Always remember that no activity is anti-spiritual or anti-yogic. Karma includes every activity, even life itself. Even at night when you sleep, you cannot renounce karma because karma is performed on many different planes, on the gross plane, on the mental and subtle planes. Even thinking is karma; it is an action.

It is true that karma yoga can be practised by going to a hospital and serving the sick, or volunteering one's services to orphanages, to lepers and blind people. It is karma yoga, but it is not the complete definition of karma yoga. One's definition of karma yoga should not be restricted to service of humanity. It must include this service, as well as a redefinition of your relationship with karma.

Efficiency in action and balance of mind

A materialistic philosophy of karma will tell us how to be happy when there is happiness and sunshine. A spiritual philosophy of karma yoga will tell us how to maintain peace of mind when everything is absolutely dark, when we have been betrayed, when we experience disloyalty and disrespect from those for whom we have sacrificed and devoted everything, in those times when we are left with the idea that life is useless or we no longer want to face it and want to escape by retiring into seclusion.

Efficiency in action coupled with balance of mind is the complete definition of karma yoga. Whenever an action is performed, it must be done with absolute awareness and with absolute efficiency. Awareness in karma yoga is essential. It is important to develop the ability to do the work in hand, while simultaneously being a witness of the actions. One must become the master of one's actions and at the same time there must be balance of mind. Aim to become a detached and disinterested observer. Though it seems to be a paradox, one is able to work more efficiently in this manner without being swayed by personal whims and prejudices, or motivated by likes or dislikes. One does whatever is necessary in the given circumstances, as they really are, without favour. In this manner one acts from the very core of one's being, the Self.

Perfection in karma yoga cannot occur until the ceaseless chattering and turmoil of the mind settles. The mind must become as clear as a crystal, as calm as a still pond. The mind must be emptied of conflict, then every action and thought will attain proper balance and the karma will become efficient. Thoughts will sometimes arise like gigantic eruptions in the endless ocean of the mind, and they will have great power, yet if one does not identify with them, they will quietly settle down into the tranquil depths again without leaving the slightest trace. Through karma yoga, the personality becomes purer and purer day by day, until unbroken peace of mind is experienced.

Create a stable base for the mind

In the path of samatvam, karma yoga is the basic sadhana because the purpose of karma yoga is to create a stable base for the mind. There are three major hurdles in spiritual experience. The first hurdle is mental impurity, the second is mental distraction and the third is mental hallucination. The hallucinations and distractions can be handled through bhakti yoga, and the impurities can be dealt with through karma yoga. In karma yoga you work for the sake of self-purification, you work in order to yoke all the tendencies of the mind, and you work with equilibrium in order to succeed in the work, but if you do not get the desired results, you should not worry.

In meditation the mind has to remain constantly on one object without the interception of another idea. However, if you keep on practising this without having attained the state of *sattwa* or balance, without having purified the mind, you will only fall back into a tamasic state. In order to prevent this, the daily activities have to be transformed through the philosophy of karma yoga.

Ego involvement

Our behaviour and feelings are related to our ego. The relationship between the ego and the circumstances of life are responsible for pain and suffering. You suffer only because of your relationships and identification with situations. Nothing in this world is a cause of suffering. You are responsible for your own sorrows. It is identification with external things which brings grief. Due to this ego you love, hate and feel happy or sad. If you are bold, it is due to ego; if you feel inferior or you are suffering from delusions of grandeur, that is also your ego.

If you can detach the ego from the situations of life and become the witness, the uninvolved silent observer, then there will be no suffering. That is true with everything in life, with human beings, business, health, relatives, lovers and friends. When there is no ego involvement, the mental reactions are different.

Therefore, along with meditation practice, studying great books, associating with saints and sages, and devotion to God, all yoga practitioners must understand their relationship with karma and redefine that relationship. For complete freedom from the eternal wheel of karma on the mental, psychic and spiritual planes, one must be able to attain and maintain equanimity of mind in all circumstances.

The path of bhakti gives peace of mind, tranquillity and one-pointedness. The path of raja yoga also gives peace of mind, one-pointedness and willpower. The path of jnana yoga, in which you rationalize and analyze, gives a clear concept of absolute reality. However, all three paths are incomplete without performing karma yoga. The day one realizes the vision of karma yoga, the life one is leading today will become a happy pilgrimage.

15

Balance between Extroversion
and Introversion

Many people with spiritual aspirations are faced with a dilemma: whether to live in the world of action, or to only practise meditational techniques. The *Ishavasya Upanishad* gives a clear answer. It says that both must be done simultaneously. One must be both extroverted and introverted, and supplement and express one's inner experience with outer actions. This is stated in no uncertain terms in verse 9: "Those who follow the path of action alone will surely enter the blinding darkness of ignorance. Furthermore, those who retreat from the world in order to seek knowledge through constant practice of meditative techniques, similarly remain in the quagmire of ignorance." This is like the razor's edge: there must be a balance between excessive worldly interest and activity, and excessive introspection, if samatvam is to be attained.

One must try to integrate the paths of extroversion and introversion. If you consider great yogis, saints and sages through history, you will realize that they all continued to express themselves in the outer world, even though they experienced the infinity of enlightenment. This applies to Buddha and Christ, to Mahatma Gandhi, Swami Vivekananda and many others. They taught their disciples, they travelled, gave sermons, and tried to help people who sought their guidance. These illumined people continued to act and express themselves in the outside world according to the natural dictates of dharma. Some became hermits; others such as Swami Sivananda and Mahatma Gandhi worked ceaselessly for the general welfare of their fellow humans. None of them became human vegetables. This applies not only to those who live in and know the highest states of illumination, it also applies to you. You too must strike a balance between external action and introspection.

The *Ishavasya Upanishad* further emphasizes this important point in verse 10: "That which is known through doing only external actions, is different to that which is known through introversion. Thus it has been said by the wise." Total concern with the outside world leads only to intellectual knowledge, not intuitive knowledge. Only by understanding the internal sphere of existence will you be able to bring about deeper understanding of the material world in which you live. On the other hand, rejection of worldly life and complete concern for meditational practices and the mind is also a block.

The reason is simple. Without resolving and harmonizing one's outer life, one can never really know deeper states of knowledge. Higher states of awareness only occur when there is perfect balance both in the inner and outer worlds. People who have a tendency to reject so-called mundane worldly activities as irrelevant to their spiritual evolution still tend to have many unresolved problems.

Dual process
Rejection of the world does not remove personality problems, which merely lie dormant in the mind, acting as obstacles to success in meditational practices. Failure to clear up the outer conflicts and concerns automatically prevents one from gaining the highest benefits from introspection. Therefore, there must be a dual process of external activities combined with periods of trying to explore the mind.

The *Bhagavad Gita* says that spiritual aspirants should never shun the active life; they must devote time to the performance of karma yoga because it is very necessary for a meditator to have some outlet for the expressions of spiritual power. If this is done, then the spiritual power generated through meditation can be practically channelled, and properly utilized and directed. In this light, all spiritual aspirants must take up the path of karma yoga, particularly in the early stages of spiritual life, for eventually there ceases to be any difference between the inner and outer world. This is what Ramana Maharshi meant when he said: "Setting apart time for meditational practices is only for beginners. A man who is advanced in the spiritual path will begin to enjoy deeper beatitude whether he is at work or not. While his hands are in society, he keeps his head cool in solitude."

However, as most aspirants are beginners it takes a combination of karma yoga, bhakti yoga, raja yoga and jnana yoga to remove the cause of tension and unhappiness, not partially, but as a whole. The human personality can be divided broadly into four fundamental categories: emotional, active, intuitive and volitional. Each person has a different temperament and inclinations according to a predominance of one or more of these traits. Accordingly, the yogic path has to be designed to suit the specific characteristics of an individual. Raja yoga is difficult; bhakti yoga is simpler, yet karma yoga is the simplest. However, that does not mean you should only do karma yoga. You must practise a synthesis of all four yogas, because in this way the paths of extroversion and introversion are integrated and emotional balance and mental peace acquired.

16

Contentment, Faith and Equanimity

Every spiritual aspirant needs to cultivate contentment of the highest order, for without it there is no possibility of holding the mind in a state of equanimity. The sadhaka will need to establish a state of constant equilibrium and stillness by a deliberate and powerful resolve or *sankalpa,* meditation, and by any other means available. The aim is to attain a state of perfect calm and serenity, no matter what happens in the external environment. The aim is not merely to acquire the ability to quell mental disturbance when it arises, but the rarer power to prevent any disturbance from taking place at all. Once a disturbance has been allowed to occur, it takes far more energy to overcome it completely. Even if outwardly it disappears quickly, the inner subconscious disturbance persists for a long time.

To reach such a state of equanimity, the aspirant needs to develop an extremely positive and dynamic state of mind, which has nothing in common with a negative mentality based on laziness and lack of initiative. It is based on perfect indifference to all personal enjoyment, comfort and other considerations that sway humanity. Its object is attainment of that peace which takes one completely beyond the realm of illusion, misery and entanglement in worldly life.

One may experience vairagya, one may believe in a higher reality and one may practise a range of sadhanas, but unless one develops a faith so strong that it does not tremble in the face of any storm whatsoever, one's commitment to yoga sadhana will remain conditional and not culminate in samatvam. Habitual behaviours developed through untold lifetimes cannot be transformed all of a sudden. Just plan and do things in an efficient and regular manner. Thinking and reasoning differ from worrying and troubling the mind. Think and decide; do not worry and tax the mind. Efficiency, intelligence and interest need be neither eliminated nor even minimized.

A faith that does not tremble

The secret of your success is that you have dedicated yourself. The reason for the failure of worldly people is that they are like logs of wood, tossed hither and thither, amidst a great ocean of problems. Do you ever wonder at the temporary vairagya which people develop for some time and which fades away very soon? It is because there is no one to help them maintain spiritual equilibrium. It is a lesson to be learned, not a matter of pity. This is how the mind behaves until it has surrendered and been cast into a pattern of tranquillity. One should have living faith in higher things. Only then can one maintain a higher degree of contentment. This is what Lord Krishna meant in the *Bhagavad Gita* when he said:

> When the perfectly controlled mind rests in the Self only, free from longing for all the objects of desires, then it is said, 'He is harmonized or balanced'. (6:18)

Everything is possible for a person who has faith, even for one whose mind has been completely shattered by the events of his life. A person with faith has very strong conviction and questions do not arise in his mind. Yet, a faithless person, a person who has doubt in his mind has no way out. One who lives in the world without a relationship with God is always in distress and without peace of mind, however much he may make a show of peace and spiritual advancement.

Therefore, always be wary of your mind, which is trying to drag you away. Do not worry about what others say or whether the world approves of you or not, and do not care for recognition or strive to be seen as important. A real devotee never murmurs, complains or grumbles over the past or present. He is able to maintain a perfect sense of balance no matter what he faces because he has seen the divine essence that supports and upholds him everywhere.

Whenever a devotee falls into difficulty, he thinks it is the Lord's grace and, therefore, he is always calm, quiet and patient, despite many stressful conditions. He does not attach much importance to the body because he knows that he is not the material body. Therefore, he is freed from the conception of false ego and is equipoised in both happiness and distress. He is tolerant and satisfied with whatever comes by the grace of God. His determination has allowed him to control his senses, to fix his awareness on his spiritual goal, and never to be swayed from devotional service. He has achieved this state of being through steadfastness in sadhana.

The contentment of a *para bhakta,* a supreme devotee, does not necessarily dawn after all his cravings have been fulfilled; rather, it is an outcome of his realization that worldly objects and events can never gratify the senses. He lives by the will of God and is thus forever content. Peace is a quality of the soul because true or everlasting peace emanates from the soul. One who is in tune with the soul has inner peace. Only one who lives by pure faith can live so freely, contented with whatever comes his way. Such a person has no worries. His mind is equipoised; he rests in the Self, forever peaceful. He has attained the yoga of equanimity, described by Lord Krishna:

> With the self unattached to external contacts, one finds happiness in the Self; with the self engaged in meditation on Brahman, one attains endless happiness. (5:21)

17

Harmonizing the Mind

Unless you are your own master, you cannot enjoy the state of equanimity. You are enslaved by your own mind, easily swayed by emotions and passions, anger and worries, unable to endure pain and sorrow, easily frustrated by difficulties and unable to rule your thoughts or command your actions. You will have to reverse this situation and attain mastery over the mind. By following the path of yoga you learn how to defeat inner enemies and achieve equanimity. Only then will you become a true yogi.

In the world today we have everything for experiencing and enjoying life, but we do not have a healthy, stable mind, a free mind, a mind with illumination and knowledge. Our external culture is highly developed, but the participants in that culture have very weak and dissipated minds. That is the main reason why people are suffering. If you honestly and impartially analyze the whole of your life, you will come to the conclusion that you have been suffering because you have not balanced your mind.

Peace of mind is most important if you want to get the most out of life, either sensual or spiritual. Think of the mind as your best friend. If you misbehave with the mind, it will create many problems. The mind is a magician. One minute it can create neurosis, in the next minute hallucinations, nervous breakdown, phobias and the desire to commit suicide. The *Bhagavad Gita* (6:6) says that the mind is your friend and also your enemy. If you learn to observe and control the mind, it will become your best friend, but if you have no understanding or control over the mind, it will be your worst enemy.

Defining the mind

Emotion, thinking, memory, feeling, reasoning, all these things with which you identify the mind, are not the total definition of the mind. The mind is a homogenous entity, an ocean of awareness, not a thinking apparatus or a bundle of habits. The mind is homogeneity of consciousness. According to Maharishi Patanjali, that which is mistaken for the mind is simply a *vritti*, a pattern, ripple or modification, not the real consciousness. An emotion is not consciousness, nor is a memory of the past or an anxiety about the future. All these feelings which we experience during sadhana or at any other time are not *chitta*, consciousness or mind, but the vrittis or modifications of the mind. When we sit for meditation practice, it is not the consciousness or the mind which we are withdrawing, but the modifications, patterns and structures of consciousness, so as to make the mind steady.

In the practice of dhyana yoga these vrittis or modifications of the mind are to be withdrawn or stopped, but in order to stop them we have to know exactly what they are composed of. Patanjali's *Yoga Sutras* states that the vrittis are fivefold: right knowledge, *pramana*; wrong knowledge, *viparyaya*; fancy or imagination, *vikalpa*; sleep, *nidra*; and memory, *smriti*. Withdraw these ripples from the surface of the mind, and then what remains is shakti. This shakti is perceived on two planes. One is *apara shakti*, energy which has been liberated from matter. The other is *atma shakti*, energy liberated from the mind. This is the ultimate essence of man.

Man is miserable because he has been unable to perceive or achieve this atma shakti, and his mind is unable to achieve a state of equipoise. Even if one is absolutely selflessly dedicated to one's work, stability of mind will not be achieved unless some time is spent every day in the practice of dhyana yoga. The mind has to be taken from outside, where it is wandering here and there among the sense objects of the world, the temporary things that are so nice in the beginning and so bad in the end, and directed inside to atma shakti, where the innermost part of the personality is full of illumination, knowledge and peace. Just sit in a quiet room and forget your accomplishments, failures, personality, social status and happiness or lack of it. After some time you will be able to understand the language of the mind, not the outer mind but the inner mind, the part of the mind that has a much greater control over our lives.

By following the process of dhyana yoga, concentration on a particular point, a process of balancing the mind is achieved. It is a process of fusion. When you sit for meditation, each thought or emotion that arises is the form of the mind and you are withdrawing it. So we have a very distinct definition of dhyana yoga. The raja yoga of Maharishi Patanjali says to withdraw the mind, concentrate the mind and then focus the whole awareness at just one point. However, if you start practising meditation directly on an object, you will have to do a lot of fighting with the mind, which may result in tension and difficulties.

First of all try to purify the nervousness, dejection and negative attitudes of the mind. Only afterwards, when you have become free from the fruits of your karma, when the karmas do not bind or affect you, when you remain untainted by your own karmas or actions, should you start meditation.

Influence of the gunas

Initially, when one tries to concentrate, the mind does not cooperate. The mind is composed of three gunas: sattwa, rajas and tamas. Those who are tamasic become lazy and fall asleep when they concentrate. Those who are rajasic by nature are not able to concentrate because the mind gallops in all directions like a wild horse. Those who are sattwic by nature are able to concentrate on the object fixed by them for some time, but then they get visions or psychic experiences, which invariably disturb the mind.

First of all, find out to which particular nature you belong. In predominantly tamasic people, the practice of meditation should be preceded by the practice of bhakti yoga and hatha yoga. Those who are predominantly rajasic by nature should not try to control the mind by force because it will only create a split in the personality. It is stated in the *Bhagavad Gita*, "Whenever this unsteady and restless mind goes out, bring it back." However, that is not possible for most of us. If we try to concentrate our mind, we will create conflict and mental chaos. Most people have to face this problem, but it can be overcome by practising with patience and perseverance.

Methods of harmonizing the mind

Maharishi Patanjali's method of yoga includes a wide range of techniques that slowly harmonize the mind and gradually induce more subtle perception, so that success in meditation practice can eventually be attained. In the *Yoga Sutras* he recommends different techniques to cater for individual temperaments so that the mind stuff can be brought into a state of peace and equilibrium. The main path of his system is contained in eight fundamental stages. The first five are the preparatory stages, or external practices of yoga: *yama*, social code, *niyama*, personal code, *asana*, sitting pose, *pranayama*, control of prana, and *pratyahara*, sense withdrawal. These five stages progressively prepare the body-mind for the last three stages: *dharana*, concentration, *dhyana*, meditation, and *samadhi*, superconsciousness. The stages up to pratyahara gradually remove external distractions, whilst the more advanced practices from dharana onwards eradicate inner disturbances from the thoughts and psychic manifestations so that the mind becomes steady and awakened to transcendental dimensions. These last three stages are the internal practices of yoga, and can only be practised successfully after mastering the earlier preparatory stages.

Yama and niyama

The yamas are designed to harmonize one's social interactions and the niyamas are intended to harmonize one's inner feelings. All the yamas and niyamas are designed to reduce friction between the outer and inner attitudes. There is a two-way relationship: the mind stimulates external actions and external actions stimulate the mind. If the external actions are not harmonious, then the mind will be disturbed. Conversely, a disturbed mind will tend to produce disharmonious acts. It is a vicious circle, where inner turmoil leads to outer turmoil and where, in turn, external turmoil leads to further inner turmoil. The yamas and niyamas aim to break this vicious circle and thereby calm the mind by adopting sensible actions and attitudes towards oneself and one's surroundings.

The five yamas are: *satya*, truthfulness, *ahimsa*, non-violence, *asteya*, honesty, *brahmacharya*, sensual control or sexual abstinence, and *aparigraha*, non-possessiveness. The five niyamas are: *shaucha*, cleanliness, *santosha*, contentment, *tapas*, austerity, *swadhyaya*, self-study, and *Ishwara pranidhana*, surrender to the cosmic will. The yamas and niyamas encompass a wide range of human activity. They tackle the problem of mental disturbance from the outer edge, the periphery, but it is also a start for more profound changes that can arise from deeper exploration of the mind. The rules are not easy to apply, but even limited application will lead to greater peace of mind. Perfect application can only arise with self-realization.

Asana

Asana is defined by Patanjali as a steady and comfortable sitting position. In theory, it can include many of the asanas of hatha yoga, but practically it includes only a few, such as padmasana and siddhasana. In Patanjali's yoga, the purpose of an asana is to balance the nerve impulses, the feelings of pain and pleasure, heat and cold, etc., to remove stress and anxiety, and to develop concentration and balance at the emotional, mental and psychic levels.

Pranayama

By manipulating the flow of breath in the nostrils using various pranayama techniques of inhalation, exhalation and retention, the practitioner can establish control over the flow of the vital energy force, and thus learn how to calm the mind and control the thought process. At an advanced level the spiritual seeker requires tranquillity of mind as an essential prelude to spiritual practice, and then pranayama can be practised to concentrate all the pranic forces of the human structure to induce one-pointedness of mind.

Pratyahara

Pratyahara means to gather inwards. The practice is concerned with checking and curbing the outgoing tendencies of the mind so that awareness can be directed inwards. It is impossible to explore the inner realms of the mind if one is addicted to, disturbed and distracted by external sense experiences. Therefore, the sense experiences, such as sound, smell, sight, touch and taste, are cut. All meditative techniques such as nada yoga, antar mouna, ajapa japa and trataka are initially concerned with inducing this stage of pratyahara. These practices have to be continued for a considerable length of time. In yoga there is no fighting with the mental impressions. The incoming impressions have to be dealt with gradually and very systematically.

At a particular point in this practice, there comes a state of introversion, where one becomes more aware of the inside and less aware of the outside. Inner experiences occur. These experiences are not an indication of spiritual enlightenment, but they prove that the mind is becoming introverted. They are psychic experiences, seeing objects, colours, light, feeling something moving in the spinal cord, and so on. When these non-empirical experiences start from within, you are ready for the next step in meditation, which is to hold your mind on one object or point.

Dharana

Dharana means concentration or one-pointedness of mind. It is the step before meditation and is concerned with fixing awareness on one object to the exclusion of all others. If the state of pratyahara has been achieved, then all outer disturbances should have been eliminated, yet the mind is still full of inner chatter in the form of memories of the past and projections of the future. The mind thinks of and tries to relive past pleasant experiences, is obsessed by unpleasant experiences or is planning or fearing the future. Therefore, it is constantly unsteady or unbalanced. Do not try to force or suppress the mind. Let it wander in and out if it wants to, but be aware that it is wandering away and bring it back to the practice again and again. In time it will grow weary of wandering and become steadier.

Various methods can be used to induce mental one-pointedness. Devotional methods try to induce it through rituals, church services, pooja or worship, chanting, kirtan, prayer and so forth. Patanjali's yoga utilizes a psychic symbol as a focal point for internal concentration. It can be one's guru, a deity, a mantra, a sound, a star, the form of a saint, an idea or a feeling, or it may be a gross object; it can be almost anything. It must however, be something that spontaneously attracts one's attention and must be chosen to suit the inherent nature of the mind and personality. The psychic symbol projected in front of the closed eyes must be so overwhelming that one's whole being is absorbed by it. Otherwise the psyche will remain scattered and balance of mind will not be possible.

During the practice of sense withdrawal and concentration, you have to work out all the perceptions and experiences in the realm of reflections, as well as in the realm of imagination or visionary experiences. If you are not prepared to exhaust the experiences amicably and with pleasure, then you will face them in the subtler form of visionary experiences. These are not spiritual experiences; they are your own samskaras, your own complexes, guilt, pride, pain and all your pathos coming out. The totality of the vrittis or modifications of consciousness that stick to you life after life and cause mental and emotional imbalances take considerable time to be discharged. It is not just a matter of two or three months. The process will take many lifetimes.

Dharana needs regular and persistent practice for a substantial period of time. In this manner the symbol or the object of concentration will help your consciousness to crystallize itself, and then when the symbol becomes clear and vivid in your imagination, the final stage of meditation comes by itself. Gradually, as the mind is harmonized, one will perceive deeper aspects of the symbol; its archetypal nature will start to reveal itself. One will spontaneously flow into dhyana.

Dhyana and samadhi

Dhyana is merely an extension of dharana. It arises when one is able to maintain a smooth, unfluctuating flow of concentration towards the inner symbol for a period of time. The mind becomes balanced as it moulds itself around one pattern in the form of the psychic symbol. The flow of awareness is often compared to a smooth flow of oil. Eventually this leads to an elimination of duality; the seer, seen and seeing merge into unity and one's being fuses into the state of samadhi.

Samadhi is the state where there is complete absence of both external and internal mental modifications; all that remains is awareness, a state of perfect balance. Samadhi brings self-realization. In the *Bhagavad Gita*, it says:

> When your mind, perplexed by what you have heard, stands immovable and steady in the Self, then you will attain Self-realization. (2:53)

During the practice of pratyahara, dharana and dhyana, whatever experiences you come across are nothing but the manifestation of the knowledge acquired by you; it is your mind facing itself, its own mindstuff. Never assume that yoga is trying to suppress the mind. The mind exists on conscious, subconscious and unconscious levels, and also in the *sthula*, gross dimension, *sukshma*, subtle dimension, as well as other dimensions. Self-awareness functions throughout and it becomes more and more effulgent and luminous when the forms, patterns and modifications that are being identified with the structure of consciousness are withdrawn. Yoga means equanimity of mind and this is achieved by control over the patterns or modifications of the mind, but not over the consciousness or the mind itself.

Chitta shuddhi

In Patanjali's yoga system cleansing all the mindstuff takes first priority. However, during the practice of pratyahara and dharana, when many impressions come up from the depths of consciousness, you try to resist them and push them back down. Whenever a thought comes into your mind you refuse to recognize it, and so because of preconceived, fixed moralities and conditioning, you are unable to face your mind. You have developed your own philosophy of puritanism which categorizes thoughts or mental impressions into good and bad. Yet it is necessary to see these thoughts also. Thousands of patterns of experiences, unworked karmas, suppressed emotions and everything else in the mindstuff, desirable and undesirable, necessary and un-necessary, horrible and wonderful, must come out. There is no other way to achieve equanimity.

Chitta shuddhi, purification of the mind, is not necessarily a pleasant or sweet process, but it is definitely a beneficial one. Through purification, the mind becomes effulgent and you are able to perceive your true nature, which is serene and peaceful. In chitta shuddhi the same type of process should occur whenever you purify the body of its foul waste matter. Naturally there is a horrible smell, but unpleasant as it is, it is necessary in the process of purifying the body. In the same manner, when purification of consciousness or *chitta* is taking place, these foul experiences also have to be faced. If you are not prepared for them, then forget raja yoga and all other yogas. No matter which yoga you practise, the toxic matter of life is going to come out. It is part of the process of samatvam.

Associated yoga techniques

The *Yoga Sutras* of Patanjali are well known, yet the eight steps are really advanced techniques for people who have exhausted most of their mental problems and conflicts. They are not really for the average person because they ask people to restrain their thoughts. For most people, who have disturbed minds, this would do more harm than good. It is only when the fluctuations of the mind are considerably fewer that one can restrain the thoughts and proceed along the path of raja yoga. One can easily crush and destroy small cockroaches that disturb the cleanliness of a yard, but it is much more difficult to tame a wild elephant. It is definitely not advisable to suppress the compelling thoughts and desires that still exist in the mind of the average person.

The basic rules of yama and niyama are also very difficult for the average person. These rules are really for people who have exhausted most of their samskaras and karmas, mental turmoil and desires. For example, if most people try to practise sexual abstinence, they will become neurotic. It can only be practised by those who have worked out most of their desires and have already purified their mind through hatha yoga, karma yoga, bhakti yoga and general meditative techniques that involve awareness more than concentration. The path of yoga formulated by Patanjali is not confined only to the eight stages. It is an integrated system that brings in many other yogic practices. One can also practise some of the associated techniques that Patanjali suggests in the *Yoga Sutras*. These methods will prepare one for the practice of the eight steps and to meet the guru who can teach them personally.

Patanjali suggests a wide range of techniques which help to harmonize one's mind and life. However, his explanations and descriptions of the techniques are very brief and terse, and it is very easy to miss the significance of Patanjali's statements without the expert guidance of a guru. Only a guru who has intimate knowledge and personal experience of yoga can point out the hidden implications behind many of the obscure verses in the *Yoga Sutras*. For example, verses 1:32–39 describe the basis of most meditative techniques, including yoga nidra, antar mouna, khechari mudra, and so on. Mantra or japa yoga is clearly indicated in verses 1:27–29. The aspirant will require clear explanations from an expert master if he is to understand how to proceed in these practices.

Maharishi Patanjali knew that the yogic path had to be designed to suit the specific characteristics of an individual. Therefore, he suggests bhakti yoga for those who are emotionally and devotionally inclined (1:23; 2:1; 2:23, 2:45; etc.). For those who are intuitive by nature he recommends jnana yoga. He recommends reflection and enquiry into the real meaning of Om (1:27–29) and also explains much of Samkhya philosophy (2:20-21 etc.) as a means to higher realization. He also makes it clear that all mental knowledge is limited.

Karma yoga for those who are active by nature is not specifically mentioned, but is implicit in many verses. For example, the yamas and niyamas imply the practice of karma yoga in daily actions and duties. Karma yoga is also implicit in the verses on bhakti yoga. Patanjali knew that success in bhakti yoga leads automatically to success in raja yoga; jnana yoga leads to perfection of raja yoga, and so forth. He knew that a person on the path of raja yoga must integrate his whole being. All the negative and limiting functions of the mind, all the petty-mindedness and egoism, have to be removed if perfect balance is to come about.

Stopping the mental modifications or vrittis can be achieved through *vairagya*, detachment, and *abhyasa*, yoga practice (1:12). This statement includes all paths and techniques of yoga. None are excluded. All lead to success in samatvam yoga.

18

Atmabhava

If you seek peace of mind for yourself only, it will not come because all around you there are problems, anxieties and restlessness. Everyone is unhappy. How can you be at peace when the whole world is in turmoil? The whole world is burning and you are seeking your own peace! First take care of others, and then take care of yourself. First take care of their peace and prosperity, and then your own peace and prosperity are guaranteed. Those who are unmoved by the sorrow of others and insensitive to their feelings can never attain peace of mind.

Everyone should realize their own flaws and failures and how their misconduct with family members is responsible for the atmosphere of inner disharmony. Nobody has the courage to face themselves as they are. You have never seen an honest reflection of yourself in the mirror. If you look into the mirror carefully, you will see an ugly reflection. You had imagined you were good-looking, but the reality is quite different.

You will realize this when you look at your behaviour and consider the treatment you mete out to your wife and your children, to your neighbours and those you work with, and to your pets and other animals. If you cannot think about others, if you cannot understand the problems of others, and if you have double standards for yourself and others, you can never attain peace of mind yourself.

Atmabhava means feeling one with others, feeling the pain, distress, poverty, sickness and calamities of others as if it were your own. Spiritual life without compassion is a waste of time. This is the sum and substance of all religions and the message of all the saints.

Extend your horizons
Yoga is a means of stilling the turbulence of the mind, of harnessing the mind and maintaining its resilience. The word *yoga* means union. Yoga is identifying yourself with the joys and sorrows of everyone, expanding your sense of selfhood, extending your horizons and rising above the pettiness of life. Identification then ceases to be personal and will win for you peace of mind. For example, if you use your money to help others, seeing no difference between one person and another, then it is aparigraha, equal vision, and an act of selflessness. It is no use developing virtues in the solitary confinement of your own home, entirely for your own spiritual progress with no benefit to society as a whole. You cannot allow yourself to be divorced from the reality of those who live around you. Those who are unmoved by the sorrow of others and insensitive to their feelings can never attain peace of mind.

If you want to attain steady wisdom and a balanced state of mind, you will need to become integrated emotionally with everyone around you. This is the message of Lord Krishna in the *Bhagavad Gita*. It is the yoga that Swami Sivananda taught. Swami Sivananda used to tell me to identify myself with the mind of a thief, of a liar, of one who spoke ill of me. His advice was, "Put yourself in their position and then you will understand them better. Your interactions with them will be peaceful and productive." If you can develop such an attitude, then the divine light of God will descend in meditation, dreams and the waking state.

Before you are able to attain peace, to experience Brahman or the Lord, to see the light or experience enlightenment, you must be able to feel the tragedy in another's

111

life. The more distant you are from the suffering of others, the further Brahman will be from you. Search for that peace which surpasses all understanding and which embraces every living creature. By taking steps to fulfil the health and prosperity of everyone, by being kind and caring to one another, the highest goal of peace of mind is within your reach. To attain yogic powers is easy, but to understand yoga is very difficult. Unless we make root and branch changes in our traditional concepts of yoga, we cannot fully bring the blessings of this wonderful science to humanity.

19

Never Barter the Peace of Your Soul

Dhau shantih antariksham shantih
Prithivee shantih aapah shantih
Aushadhayah shantih vanaspathayah shantih
Purusha shantih brahma shantih
Sarvam shantih shantireva shantih
Shantih me astu shantih.
Om shantih shantih shantih

Peace in heaven, peace in space,
Peace on earth, peace in the waters,
Peace to the herbs, peace to the plants and trees,
Peace to the indweller, peace to the Creator,
Peace to all, peace, only peace.
Peace will give (me) peace.
Om Shantih Shantih Shantih

Everyone is searching for inner peace. Human beings know the ways of worldly life and can obtain everything they seek in that life. But the most precious thing needed today is inner peace. What is inner peace? Is she a damsel? Is she an idea? Is she an experience? How can peace of mind be found?

When we say *Om Shantih Shantih Shantih*, it is for peace of the total mind: the conscious mind, the subconscious mind and the unconscious mind, which we do not know. Peace in the conscious mind means peace upon earth. Peace in the subconscious mind means peace in the skies or beneath the earth. Then there is peace in heaven and peace everywhere. This is the peace 'that passeth all understanding'. It is not the peace of mind where you delude yourself by taking a few tranquillizers and have a good night's sleep, or about the peace you enjoy momentarily when one or two of your desires have been temporarily satisfied.

The search for peace

Whether we are Hindus, Christians or Muslims, whether we are rich or poor, men or women, we are all searching for *shanti*, peace. Everyone's peace of mind has been hijacked. We feel disturbed. Where has our peace of mind gone? Far, far away is the answer. But where is that 'far far away'? Has shanti gone to England or has she gone to the Netherlands? Has she gone far, far away to China? Who has kidnapped her? This is the problem we sing about during chanting of the *Ramacharita-manas*. The mantras tell of the monkey Hanuman who flies across the ocean to find out where peace has been hidden. He finds her lying captive. Sita, the symbol of supreme peace, has been kidnapped by the ten-headed demon, Ravana.

Everyone wants peace, and this peace is Sita who has been kidnapped by our ten senses and kept as a prisoner in golden Lanka. Our peace has not gone somewhere within us, nor has someone else disturbed our peace. We alone have disturbed it; we ourselves are responsible. Our peace has vanished because we have become the slave of our ten senses. We have kidnapped shanti and become a slave of tensions and worries. This ten-headed monster lives in a palace. Ten-headed Ravana lives in a city of gold. And whose is that citadel? Your own body is the citadel where peace of mind has been held captive. It means that you have to search for peace within your own self.

Therefore, the first truth is that you have hijacked peace. Secondly, that peace has to be sought within you, not outside. This is the sum and substance of what people sing about so gladly when they chant the *Ramacharitamanas*.

Inner peace

Inner peace is of utmost importance; it is a pure state of mind. In this state of equanimity the mind is active and alert, but it does not act as a partner to worldly events. Sleep and lethargy do not represent inner peace. Forgetfulness is not inner peace. Inner peace is not a state of unawareness of external or internal events. Inner peace is far beyond inertia. Proper understanding is inner peace. Having obtained inner peace, one becomes powerful. When one is established in inner peace, nothing can shake the soul.

We lose our mental balance because we become partners in the events of life, because we become interested in and attached to everyone and everything we come across. In short, we lose our inner peace when we identify with worldly happenings. The aspirant who is established in equanimity does not allow himself to be influenced by his environment, nor by the effects of his ten senses, nor by what is agreeable and disagreeable to them. Of course, in order to retain and experience that inner peace one must have strength. Divine bliss and joy demand inner strength.

To experience inner peace, one must prepare the mind. As long as the senses wander amongst sensual objects seeking satisfaction, there will be no inner peace. To attain inner peace, firstly the mind must be withdrawn from the senses and, secondly, it must be kept united with the highest purpose of existence. Through this inner and outer control the wisdom of the devotee becomes unwavering and steady, and does not hover between divine and sensual pleasures.

When you assert that you are the blissful soul, equipoised in every condition of life, you must live up to your claims. You must realize it. You must experience it. So begin to practise any mantras of your choice without inhibition. It may be Om, Rama or Gayatri. Combine your mantra with pranayama and bandhas to accelerate the effect. Learn the three stages of pranayama: *pooraka,* inhalation, *kumbhaka,* retention, and *rechaka,* exhalation. Practise in a comfortable sitting asana. Siddhasana/siddha yoni asana is best, followed by padmasana, vajrasana and swastikasana. Practise bandhas at the time of breath retention. Adjust the mantra with inhalation and exhalation in the ratio of 1:2. If you inhale for one unit of Gayatri, then you must exhale for two units. Five rounds of this pranayama coupled with bandhas and mantra will give sufficient experience of dhyana. These fifteen to twenty minutes every day will go a long way to bringing inner peace and unity into your personality.

Inner peace brings equanimity

Inner peace is obtainable through God's grace. Happiness, sorrow, disease, poverty and suffering are all part of life's experiences, but grace is different. Lord Rama experienced suffering. Lord Krishna passed through suffering. All the saints had to face suffering and they accepted it, because by doing so they were able to receive the grace of God. God's grace is the one thing present in every situation, but can you see it? Wherever there is grace, there is inner peace. That is why our rishis and munis always sought ways to obtain His grace.

Man is the most beautiful and privileged creation of God, yet pain and pleasure may come his way. The clouds of calamities may eclipse your inner shrine, but with nothing should you barter the peace of your soul. Peace, contentment, equanimity and steadiness of mind should be your life! Only one who considers pain and pleasure as passing clouds and is always aware of his goal will be really happy. Whenever you get time, peep within and experience the stillness and silence of your soul. We all are pilgrims here.

Spiritual aspirants must know how to maintain equanimity under all circumstances and be able to sustain the contentment and peace inherent in that state of mind. The self, the mind, heart, intentions and actions can be purified and balanced through karma yoga. This will give peace of mind. Practising yoga will evolve the consciousness, improve the quality of awareness and enable you to realize that you are not the body, but something more than that. If the

116

thoughts become calm and quiet and if you are able to think, decide and solve the problems of your life with absolute tranquillity, that is samatvam yoga.

Side by side with yoga practise divine life, little by little. Practise *ahimsa,* non-violence, *satya,* truthfulness, *brahmacharya,* celibacy, *aparigraha,* non-possessiveness, *asteya,* honesty, *shaucha,* cleanliness, *santosha,* contentment, and so on. Accept pain and suffering. Do not be afraid of pain. Do not depend on the things of the world as your security in life. Your real security is being able to face everything with a balanced mind.

Glossary

Adharma – disharmony, unrighteousness

Ahamkara – ego; awareness of existence of 'I'

Ahimsa – absence of violence from the personality

Ajapa japa – meditation practice in which mantra is coordinated with the breath; a powerful technique for sense withdrawal which can induce concentration and deep meditation

Anasakti – non-attachment, dispassion

Antar mouna – inner silence; meditative technique belonging to the fifth step of raja yoga (pratyahara)

Anushthana – a resolve to perform sadhana with absolute discipline for a required period of time

Aparigraha – freedom from covetousness; without possessions or belongings; one of the five yamas described in raja yoga

Arjuna – in the Bhagavad Gita he received divine wisdom from Lord Krishna

Artha – attainment in all spheres of life; material need; one of the four purusharthas

Asana – physical posture in which one is at ease and in harmony; steady and comfortable meditation posture

Atma – pure consciousness; soul or inner spirit; the universal atma (paramatma) manifests as the individual atma (jivatma)

Atma anubhuti – experience of the inner self or atma

Atmabhava – feeling unity with all; seeing the atman equally in all beings

Atma chintan – self-introspection; constant contemplation on the self

Atma jnana – knowledge of the self

Atma shakti – spiritual force of energy

Avidya – ignorance

Bhagavad Gita – one of the best loved and most practical scriptures in which Lord Krishna explains the eighteen types of yoga; part of the historical epic Mahabharata

Bhakta – devotee

Bhakti – intense inner devotion or love

Bhava – feeling; love; inclination or disposition of mind

Brahma – creator of the universe

Brahma vidya – knowledge of the self

Brahmacharya – redirection of sexual energy towards spiritual and meditative experience; living in constant awareness of Brahman

Brahmacharya ashrama – first stage of life to twenty-five years of age, devoted to learning and study

Brahman – supreme self; eternal principle of existence or ultimate reality

Buddhi – discerning, discriminative aspect of mind

Chitta – individual consciousness; storehouse of samskaras or archetypes

Chitta shuddhi – purification of the mind

Dama – restraint of the senses

Darshan – to see; spiritual vision; to have inner vision or blessing of the divine power

Deva(i) – divine being

Dharana – concentration

Dharma – natural role one has to play in life; duty; righteous action; one of the four purusharthas

Dhyana – meditation, constant total awareness

Dvandvas – pairs of opposites

Dwesha – aversion, dislike

Ekanta – alone, by oneself, solitary

Grihastha – householder

Grihastha ashrama – second stage of life; married, householder life from twenty-five to fifty years

Guna – quality; three attributes present in all creation: tamas, rajas and sattwa

Guru – dispeller of darkness; spiritually enlightened soul who by the grace of his own atma can dispel darkness, ignorance and illusion from the mind of a disciple

Hanuman – name of a powerful monkey chief who played a very important role in the Ramayana as Lord Rama's great devotee

Hatha yoga – system of yoga specifically dealing with practices for physical and mental purification

Iccha – desire

Ida nadi – major pranic/psychic channel in the subtle body which conducts mental energy throughout the body and mind, located on the left side of the body

Indriyas – ten sense organs of cognition and action

Ishavasya Upanishad – Ishavasya literally means 'enveloped by God'; an Upanishad concerned with the supreme knowledge of divine immanence and all-pervasiveness

Ishta devata – tutelary deity; one's personal symbol; form or vision of divinity

Ishwara – Lord, God; pure consciousness

Japa – conscious and continual repetition of mantra

Jivanmukta - one who is liberated while living, who feels that all is Brahman only, and who is taintless

Jivatma – individual soul

Jnana – true knowledge; wisdom

Jnana yoga – yoga of knowledge and wisdom attained through self-analysis and investigation of abstract or speculative ideas

Jnanendriyas – five sensory organs of knowledge: ears, eyes, nose, tongue, skin

Kama – emotional need for fulfilment; one of the four purusharthas

Karma – action; law of cause and effect that shapes the destiny of each individual

Karma yoga – perfection in action; action performed with meditative awareness; yoga of dynamic meditation; yogic path of selfless service

Karmendriyas – five organs of action: hands, feet, tongue, excretory and reproductive organs

Krishna – eighth incarnation of Lord Vishnu, the cosmic sustainer; the principal figure of the Bhagavad Gita

Kundalini – vital force or latent energy residing in mooladhara chakra, often referred to as the serpent power

Laya yoga – yoga of conscious dissolution of individuality

Manas – rational aspect of mind which creates thought/counter thought

Mandukya Upanishad – one of the principal Upanishads describing the states of consciousness represented by the sacred letters composing the mantra Om

Mantra – subtle sound or combination of sound vibrations used for liberating consciousness from the limitations of mundane awareness

Maya – creative power; power of illusion

Moksha – liberation from the cycles of birth, death and rebirth; inner freedom; one of the four purusharthas

Mumukshutva – intense longing for liberation

Muni -- one who maintains silence or stillness of mind

Nada yoga – yogic technique using subtle inner sounds to penetrate deeper and deeper into the nature of one's own reality

Nirguna Brahman – formless God

Nirvana – enlightenment; samadhi; harmony between the individual consciousness and universal consciousness

Nirvikalpa samadhi – the highest superconscious state where all mental modifications cease to exist and only pure consciousness remains

Nishkama karma yogi – one who dedicates all actions to God

Niyama – observances or rules of personal discipline to render the mind tranquil in preparation for meditation

Om – cosmic vibration of the universe; universal mantra; represents four states of mind: conscious, subconscious, unconscious and supraconscious or cosmic mind

Paripurna – constantly full

Prakriti – active principle of the manifest world; mother nature

Prana – vital energy force, essence of life

Pranayama – a series of techniques using the breath to control the flow of prana within the body; expansion of the range of vital energy

Pratipaksha bhavana – yogic principle of controlling a negative emotion by summoning its opposite

Pratyahara – withdrawal and emancipation of the mind from the senses

Purusha – pure consciousness; the indweller

Purushartha – personal effort; four areas of human endeavour to be fulfilled: artha, kama, dharma and moksha

Raja yoga – eightfold path classified by Maharshi Patanjali in the *Yoga Sutras*

Rajas – one of the three gunas, representing the dynamic, active state of mind and nature

Ramacharitamanas – a version of the Ramayana written in a Hindi dialect by Tulsidas

Ravana - ten-headed demon king of Lanka; his ten heads symbolize attachment via the five karmendriyas and five jnanendriyas

Sadhaka – one who practices sadhana; spiritual aspirant; a seeker

Sadhana – spiritual practice done regularly for attainment of inner experience and self-realization

Saguna Brahman – God with form

Sama drishti – equal vision

Samadhana – mental equilibrium, mental balance; the fruit of the practice of sama, dama, uparati, titiksha and shraddha; fixing the mind on the Atman

Samadhi – culmination of meditation; final step of raja yoga; self-realization

Samsara – the process of worldly life

Samskara – unconscious memories; past mental impressions which set up impulses and trains of thought; an impression in the subconscious mind

Sankalpa – will, positive resolve; thought

Sannyasa – renunciation; dedication; from sam meaning 'equable', and nyasa meaning 'trust'

Sanyam – action with discrimination, detachment, self-restraint

Satsang – gathering of spiritually minded people, in which the ideals and principals of truth are discussed; spiritual association

Sattwa – one of the three gunas representing harmony, equilibrium, steadiness and purity

Shadsampat – sixfold virtues: shama, dama, uparati, titiksha, shraddha and samadhana

Shama – tranquil, equipoise, calmness of mind

Shanti – peace, inner serenity, tranquillity

Shraddha – faith

Sita – symbol of supreme peace; the wife of Lord Rama in the Ramayana, and the heroine who was captured by the demon king Ravana

Sushumna – the chief of the astral tubes in the body running inside the spinal column

Swabhava – one's inherent nature which is bliss and equipoise; therefore one seeks to re-attain that state

Swadhyaya – self-study, self-analysis, self-awareness

Tamas – one of the three gunas, representing inertia, dullness

Trataka – concentration practice of gazing with unblinking eyes at one point to focus the mind

Titiksha – power of endurance

Turiya – supraconscious state beyond the realm of the gunas; the unmanifest state of pure consciousness

Uparati – indifference; desisting from worldliness; abstaining from sensual enjoyments

Vairagya – dispassion; detachment, non-attachment; state in which one is internally calm and tranquil amidst the tumultuous events of the world

Vanaprastha – forest-dweller, the third of the four vedic stages of life

Vasana – seed or latent inherent desire

Vedanta – end of the Vedas, the school of thought based primarily on the vedic upanishads

Viveka – right understanding, higher discrimination, indirect knowledge or intuition

Vrittis – modifications of mind

Yama – self-restraints or rules of conduct which render the emotions tranquil

Yoga – union; a systematic science of the body and mind leading to the union of the individual consciousness with the universal or cosmic consciousness

Yoga Sutras – ancient authoritative text on raja yoga by Maharishi Patanjali